Clues to Comprehension
Building Strategic Thinking Skills Through Language Play

Riddle Posters

In *Clues to Comprehension*, 40 posters present riddles to solve that engage students in critical and deductive thinking as they try to determine the identity of the "mystery item" that is the subject of each poster. The mystery items come from categories that range from "nursery rhyme characters" and "community helpers" to "places in the community," "animals," and more.

Teacher Pages

For each poster, an accompanying teacher's page provides guidelines for modeling and practicing critical-thinking strategies. As you conduct these lessons, encourage students to explain the thinking behind their responses. Accept all answers that can be logically substantiated by students, even though they may at first appear to be incorrect or inaccurate. It may turn out that a student is thinking "outside the box" or using a perspective that may be different from yours and other students'.

Student Pages

A reproducible student page is also included for each of the 40 lessons. These pages use item formats similar to those found on many standardized language skills tests, and include skills such as vocabulary development, reading comprehension, decoding, and structural analysis.

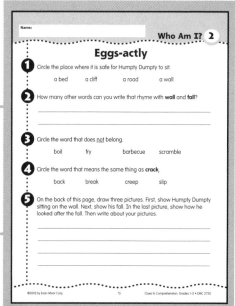

Model Use of Picture Clues

As you guide students through the steps in the **Use Picture Clues** section, model how to work with the nontext clues provided in the illustrations. Encourage students to focus first on the illustration—not the text—and to use logic and deductive reasoning to support their hypotheses.

Model Use of Text Clues

As you lead students through the steps outlined under **Use Text Clues**, encourage students to use new information to revise their hypotheses. Again, always have students explain their reasoning, and accept all answers that can be supported with logic.

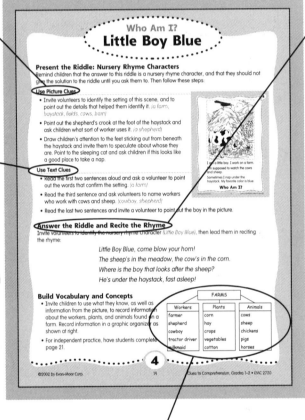

Confirm Solutions and Share Information

As you move into the **Answer the Riddle** section, encourage students to share information they have on the subject under discussion. To ensure best use of discussion time, establish guidelines for participating in class discussions. These might include:

- Raise your hand and wait to be recognized before speaking.
- Give others your full attention while they are speaking.
- Respect everybody's right to hold individual opinions, whether you agree with them or not.
- Try to support your statements with examples or logic.

Model Critical Thinking with Graphic Organizers

Graphic organizers make critical thinking "visible" for students. By using "think-alouds" as you work with the graphic organizers in the **Build Vocabulary and Concepts** activities, you can help students understand how to think about organizing, interpreting, and understanding information.

Use the graphic organizer templates provided on pages 132–141 to create overhead transparencies, or copy the sample organizers on the teacher pages onto the chalkboard or chart paper.

As you write, share your thought process with students by talking through the reasoning behind the organizational structure you are modeling. When you make your thinking explicit by verbalizing it to students, you help them begin to internalize principles for organizing information. As you progress through the 40 lessons, encourage students to suggest organizational structures. Ask questions such as, *"If we want to look at the way two things are similar and different, what would be a good way to organize our information?"*

The activities on the reproducible student pages use the content of the posters as a springboard to related language arts activities. Activity formats emulate many of the typical item formats found on standardized language tests. You can help students feel prepared and confident when they encounter items of this type by modeling and reviewing strategies for approaching each type of activity. See pages 6 and 7 for tips on teaching the following skills, which are presented on the student pages:

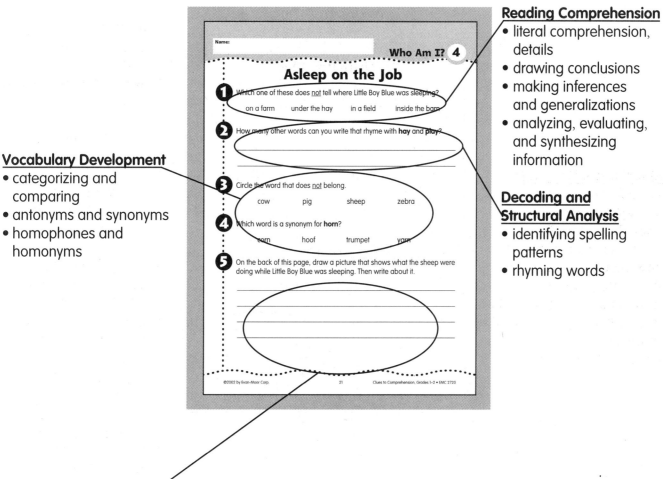

Reading Comprehension
• literal comprehension, details
• drawing conclusions
• making inferences and generalizations
• analyzing, evaluating, and synthesizing information

Decoding and Structural Analysis
• identifying spelling patterns
• rhyming words

Vocabulary Development
• categorizing and comparing
• antonyms and synonyms
• homophones and homonyms

Open-Ended Exercises

On each activity page, there is also an open-ended item that asks students to draw and write in response to a prompt. Students are often asked to use the back side of the student activity pages to draw in response to a prompt. Drawing first helps students focus their thoughts in a way that is usually nonthreatening. Then when students are asked to write about their picture, they already have a visual guide to help get them started in their writing.

Use the writing samples to track the aspects of writing that you wish to evaluate or focus on for individual or group instruction.

See page 8 for ideas for meeting the needs of students acquiring English and accelerated and struggling learners.

About the CD-ROM

Loading the Program

1 Put the CD in your CD drive.

This CD-ROM contains both Windows and MacOS programs.

Your computer will recognize the correct program.

2 On some computers, the program will automatically start up. If the program does not start automatically:

Windows—go to My Computer, double click on the CD drive, then double click on Begin.exe.

MacOS—double click on the CD icon on your desktop, then double click on Begin.

3 After the program starts, you will arrive at the main menu.

Main Menu Features

The 40 riddles found in the book are presented in full-color with an interactive element. To present a whole-class lesson, connect your computer to a projection system. As a review, students may be taught to access a specific riddle during their computer time.

○ Choose a Topic

1 Click on **Choose a Topic** to display the list of categories.

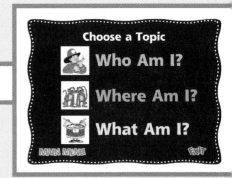

2 Click on a topic. The topic will be displayed, along with riddle numbers.

3 Click on a riddle number. The riddle number will be displayed, followed by a full-color illustration of a picture from the book. For example, **#1, Who Am I? Little Bo Peep.**

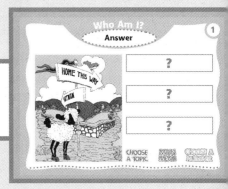

4

Refer to Riddle #1 in the workbook, **Who Am I?, Little Bo Peep**, and follow the directions in the book.

Click on the first **?**.

The first riddle clue accompanying the illustration will be displayed. The clues are set up to follow the directions in the **Use Text Clues** section on the teacher page in the book. Proceed to click on the second **?**, and then the third to reveal all of the text riddle clues.

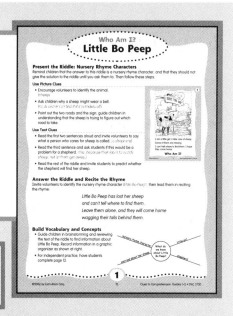

5

After discussing the clues and possible solutions, click on to reveal the answer.

6

You may then click on CHOOSE A NUMBER to select the next riddle number, and repeat steps #3 through #5,

or you may click on CHOOSE A TOPIC to select another category, or click on EXIT to close the program.

View the E-Book

The teacher pages, riddle posters, activity pages, and answer key are presented in a printable electronic format. You must have Adobe® Acrobat® Reader™ installed to access the e-book. (See installation instructions below.)

Installing Adobe® Acrobat® Reader™
You need to have Acrobat Reader installed on your computer to access the e-book portion of the CD-ROM. If you do not have Acrobat Reader, go to the main menu of the CD and follow these instructions:

1. Place your cursor over the Click Here link. Wait for the hand and then click.
2. When you see the Acrobat Reader Setup Screen, click the "Next" box.
3. When you see the Destination Location Screen, click the "Next" box.
4. When you see the Setup Complete Screen, click "finish."

Your system will now shut down to finish the installation process. Some systems will automatically restart. If yours does not, start it up manually.

You may scroll through the entire book page by page or open the "Bookmarks" tab for a clickable table of contents.

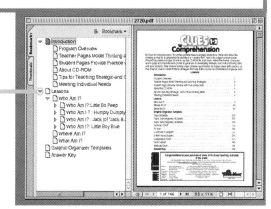

Hint: This symbol, ⊞ for Windows or ▷ for MacOS, means that you can click there to expand this category.

To print pages from the e-book, click on the printer icon. A print dialog box will open. Enter the page or pages you wish to print in the print range boxes. (At the bottom of the screen, you can see which page of the e-book you are viewing.)

To exit the e-book, simply "X" out until you return to the main menu.

Exit. This button closes the program.

Tips for Teaching Strategic- and Critical-Thinking Skills

Rhyming Words and Spelling Patterns

For activities that ask students to write rhyming words, teach students to make alphabet strips and model how to use them with word cards to find rhyming words as shown at right.

As students begin to learn initial blends and clusters, guide them in creating blend strips to help them expand their universe of possible rhyming words.

Use the rhyming word activities to help students focus on the various spelling patterns that represent the same sound. For example, in searching for words that rhyme with *peep*, you may want to point out the rhyming word *leap*, then invite students to use their alphabet strips to find additional rhyming words that use the *-eap* spelling pattern.

You may also compile the rhyming words recorded by students on their activity pages and display them on bulletin boards or in the writing center as resources for students. Rhyming word collections are especially helpful for writing poetry.

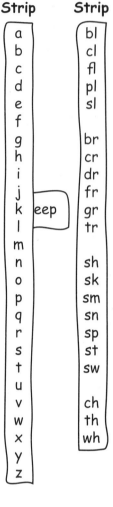

Synonyms and Antonyms

You may not feel the need to teach your students these terms immediately, but may prefer to describe them as "words that mean the same thing" and "words that mean the opposite" of the target words presented in these exercises.

Teach students to use word-substitution strategies for synonym and antonym exercises. Use think-alouds that first put the target word into a context sentence, and then substitute the answer choices to find the correct answer (see #3 on page 12):

> *We're trying to find a word that means the opposite of* lost. *First, let's use* lost *in a sentence: Little Bo Peep* lost *her sheep. Now, let's substitute the other words for* lost *in that sentence: Little Bo Peep* missing *her sheep. No,* missing *is similar to* lost, *not the opposite. OK, Little Bo Peep* last *her sheep. No, that doesn't make sense. Little Bo Peep* found *her sheep. Yes, that is the opposite of* lost. *Let's just check the last choice: Little Bo Peep* most *her sheep. No, that doesn't make sense either, so* found *is definitely the correct answer.*

Use a similar procedure to model how to check whether words are synonyms.

No, *missing* is similar to *lost*, not the opposite.

Categorization

Most activity pages include an exercise that requires students to identify a word that does not fit in the same category as three other words. Be sure to model the strategy for approaching this sort of exercise by using think-alouds to identify the category and the element that does not fit (see #3 on page 12):

We need to find the word that does <u>not</u> belong in this group. First, we need to see what this group is. What group do sheep, bull, lamb, *and* ram *all belong to? You are right: They are all animals. And* sheep, lamb, *and* ram *are all in the same animal family. A lamb is a baby sheep, and a ram is a male sheep. Is a bull in this family? No, so that is the word that does <u>not</u> belong.*

Make sure students have plenty of practice working through this sort of exercise as part of a teacher-directed group before you expect them to feel comfortable completing such exercises on their own. Encourage students to continue to identify the reasoning for their decisions even when they work independently.

Comprehension Exercises

Several types of exercises on the student pages require students to process information from the poster text in order to answer literal comprehension questions, make generalizations and inferences, and draw conclusions.

Other exercises require students to apply similar critical-thinking skills to topics that have been explored during teacher-directed discussions. For example, on the student page for Lesson 5, the first comprehension exercise requires students to make inferences about the story of "The Three Little Pigs" (see #1 on page 24). The story itself is not presented on the poster, but rather is discussed by the group as part of building concepts and vocabulary.

In modeling strategies for conducting comprehension activities, use think-alouds to show how to examine each answer option, using critical thinking, deductive reasoning, text clues, and other traditional reading comprehension strategies to select the correct answer choices. Once again, encourage students to support their answer choices with logical reasoning, bearing in mind that students may be able to justify an answer that might otherwise appear to be incorrect to you or to other students. (Note that the answer key often specifies "Accept all appropriate responses" for this sort of item.)

Meeting Individual Needs

Students Acquiring English

Clues to Comprehension can be easily adapted to further enhance acquisition of concepts and vocabulary for students who are acquiring English as a second language. Consider these simple modifications, which may also provide extra support for native English speakers who are struggling readers:

- **Teach Cultural Literacy**—Be sure to include "cultural literacy" instruction in lessons that feature nursery rhyme characters, traditional folktales, American holidays, or other elements that may be culture-specific. This is a great opportunity for helping non-native English speakers fill in gaps in basic American cultural literacy.

- **Provide Visual Clues**—As you capture information shared by students during group discussions or as you develop graphic organizers, add simple sketches to help students quickly grasp the meaning of new or unfamiliar words.

- **Highlight Sound/Symbol Correspondence**—Whenever you model writing for students, verbalize each word as you write it. This helps increase students' awareness of the letters that are used to represent particular sounds.

- **Capitalize on Teachable Moments**—As you lead student discussions, create graphic organizers, or work through student exercises, be sure to take advantage of any teachable moments that arise to make connections for students. You may wish to refer to vocabulary introduced previously as you explain the meaning of a new synonym that comes up during a discussion. Or, you may wish to make a point about spelling rules by using a word that comes up to introduce a family of words that all include a unique spelling pattern. Teachable moments are impossible to predict, but invaluable to deepening students' understanding of new concepts, vocabulary, and rules.

Struggling and Accelerated Learners

With its format of guided discussion and individual follow-up activities, *Clues to Comprehension* provides an ideal structure for allowing students at varying ability levels to participate in enriching experiences together. Whether as active participants or silent observers, all students can benefit from the group discussion format. As students become proficient in using the various learning strategies to complete the student activity pages, you may allow accelerated learners to move ahead on their own in completing these pages, while you work with a smaller group to focus on identifying and applying learning strategies for each exercise.

Consider any of these possibilities for extending learning for accelerated students:

- Have students use the rhyming words that they brainstorm to compose a rhyme or poem.

- Write sentences or definitions for the rhyming words that they list.

- Identify the category that items belong to in the categorization activities.

- Invite students to identify and explain humorous elements in the poster art and text.

Struggling learners should be supported through ongoing instruction and review of the learning strategies modeled in the program until they feel comfortable using them independently. Encourage struggling writers to dictate text to accompany their drawings in the open-ended writing activity. They may also add labels to their pictures, then slowly build up to writing simple sentences.

Who Am I?

I am oval-shaped.
I am a kind of food.
My shell can crack if I fall.
I should never sit on walls. The king's men could not put me together again.

Who Am I?

I am a little girl. I take care of sheep.
Some of them are missing.
I can't tell where to find them. I hope they come home.

Who Am I?

...m a boy. I carry a pail. I took a ...k to get some water.
I fell down a hill and hurt my head.
I have a friend named Jill.

Who Am I?

Present the Riddle: Nursery Rhyme Characters

Remind children that the answer to this riddle is a nursery rhyme character, and that they should not give the solution to the riddle until you ask them to. Then follow these steps:

Use Picture Clues

- Encourage volunteers to identify the animal.
  (sheep)

- Ask children why a sheep might wear a bell.
  (so its owner can find it if it wanders off)

- Point out the two roads and the sign; guide children in understanding that the sheep is trying to figure out which road to take.

Use Text Clues

- Read the first two sentences aloud and invite volunteers to say what a person who cares for sheep is called. *(a shepherd)*

- Read the third sentence and ask students if this would be a problem for a shepherd. *(Yes, because their job is to watch sheep, not let them get away.)*

- Read the rest of the riddle and invite students to predict whether the shepherd will find her sheep.

I am a little girl. I take care of sheep.
Some of them are missing.
I can't tell where to find them. I hope they come home.

Who Am I?

Answer the Riddle and Recite the Rhyme

Invite volunteers to identify the nursery rhyme character *(Little Bo Peep)*, then lead them in reciting the rhyme:

> *Little Bo Peep has lost her sheep*
> *and can't tell where to find them.*
> *Leave them alone, and they will come home*
> *wagging their tails behind them.*

Build Vocabulary and Concepts

- Guide children in brainstorming and reviewing the text of the riddle to find information about Little Bo Peep. Record information in a graphic organizer as shown at right.

- For independent practice, have students complete page 12.

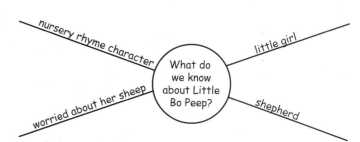

nursery rhyme character
little girl
What do we know about Little Bo Peep?
worried about her sheep
shepherd

1

Clues to Comprehension, Grades 1–2 • EMC 2720

Asleep on the Job

1 Which one of these does <u>not</u> tell where Little Boy Blue was sleeping?

    on a farm   under the hay   in a field   inside the barn

2 How many other words can you write that rhyme with **hay** and **play**?

_____

_____

3 Circle the word that does <u>not</u> belong.

    cow   pig   sheep   zebra

4 Which word is a synonym for **horn**?

    corn   hoof   trumpet   yarn

5 On the back of this page, draw a picture that shows what the sheep were doing while Little Boy Blue was sleeping. Then write about it.

_____

_____

_____

_____

Who Am I?
The Wolf
(of "The Three Little Pigs")

Present the Riddle: Fairy Tale Characters

Remind children that the answer to this riddle is a fairy tale character, and that they should not give the solution to the riddle until you ask them to. Then follow these steps:

Use Picture Clues

- Ask volunteers to describe the setting. Is it the city, the countryside, the beach, a forest? *(a forest)*

- Point out the house and ask children to speculate about what it is made of *(bricks)* and who might live there. *(Answers will vary.)*

- Point out the eyes peering out from the edge of the forest and ask children whose they might be, and whether they look friendly or scary.

Use Text Clues

- Read the first two sentences and ask a volunteer to point out the part of the animal that is visible in the picture. *(the eyes)*

- Read the last two sentences and have a volunteer point out the brick house.

I am big and furry. I am a forest animal.

My neighbors are three brother pigs. They all live in a brick house.

Who Am I?

Answer the Riddle and Tell the Tale

Invite volunteers to identify the fairy tale character *(the wolf from "The Three Little Pigs")*.

Ask volunteers to summarize the tale.

(Three pig brothers set out to build their homes. The first builds his of straw, the second of sticks, and the third of bricks. The wolf blows down the first two houses, but the pigs are saved when they run to the third brother's house. The wolf cannot blow the brick house down. When he tries to get in by going down the chimney, he gets cooked in a pot of boiling water that the clever pigs had heated in the fireplace.)

Build Vocabulary and Concepts

- Guide children in brainstorming words to describe the wolf and the pigs. Record them in a T-chart as shown at right.

- For independent practice, have students complete page 24.

Wolf	Pigs
bully	brave
big and furry	small and pink
hungry	scared
lives in forest	live in brick house
mean	clever
long, furry tail	short, curly tails

5

Who Am I?
An Astronaut

Present the Riddle: Workers

Remind children that the answer to this riddle is the name of a type of worker, and that they should not give the solution to the riddle until you ask them to. Then follow these steps:

Use Picture Clues

Prompt discussion by asking: What do you see in this picture?
(space shuttle, spaceship, rocket, Earth, planets, stars, space, etc.)

Use Text Clues

- Read the first two sentences aloud and ask children to speculate about the identity of this worker.

- Read the next two sentences and encourage students to revise their hypotheses.

- Read the last sentence.

I can be a man or a woman. I travel to faraway places.

I have to wear a special suit and helmet. I fly high above Earth.

I can visit the Moon in my rocket.

Who Am I?

Answer the Riddle and Discuss Astronauts

Invite volunteers to identify the worker *(an astronaut)* and to share any other information they have about astronauts.

Build Vocabulary and Concepts

- Guide children in using information from the riddle and group discussion to complete a graphic organizer about astronauts as shown below.

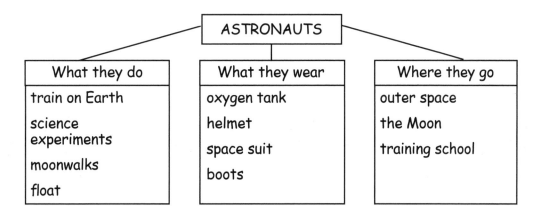

- For independent practice, have students complete page 27.

I can be a man or a woman. I travel to faraway places.

I have to wear a special suit and helmet. I fly high above Earth.

I can visit the Moon in my rocket.

Who Am I?

Blast Off!

1 Choose the best word to complete this sentence:

Astronauts can blast off to the _____.

| clouds | Earth | Moon | ocean |

2 Circle the word that does <u>not</u> rhyme with **Moon**.

spoon   Mom   June   tune

3 Which one <u>cannot</u> be an **astronaut**?

a man   a woman   a boy   a scientist

4 Circle the word that means the opposite of **far**.

away   fear   for   near

5 Imagine you are an astronaut on a trip to the Moon. On the back of this page, draw a picture to show what you see and do. Then write about it.

_____

_____

_____

Who Am I?
A Waitress

Present the Riddle: Workers

Remind children that the answer to this riddle is the name of a type of worker, and that they should not give the solution to the riddle until you ask them to. Then follow these steps:

Use Picture Clues

Invite volunteers to identify the setting in this picture, and to name the things that helped them figure it out. *(a restaurant; menu, stools at counter, meal carried on a tray)*

Use Text Clues

- Read the first two sentences aloud and invite volunteers to name women workers who wear uniforms. *(nurse, doctor, police officer, firefighter, etc.)*

- Read the third sentence and invite students to revise their hypotheses.

- Read the rest of the riddle and invite volunteers to point out the words that gave them the best clues about this worker.

I am a woman. I wear a uniform.
I work at a restaurant.
I take your order and bring you your food. It's nice when you leave a tip for me.

Who Am I?

Answer the Riddle and Discuss Waitresses

Invite volunteers to identify the worker *(a waitress)* and to share any other information they have about waitresses. Ask volunteers to explain what a tip is and how tipping works.

Build Vocabulary and Concepts

- Guide children in comparing two restaurant workers and their jobs. Record their comments in two columns, then reorganize them into a Venn diagram as shown below.

- For independent practice, have students complete page 30.

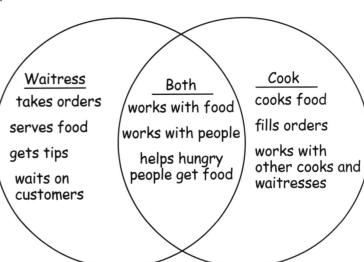

Waitress
takes orders
serves food
gets tips
waits on customers

Both
works with food
works with people
helps hungry people get food

Cook
cooks food
fills orders
works with other cooks and waitresses

7

Present the Riddle: Workers

Remind children that the answer to this riddle is the name of a type of worker, and that they should not give the solution to the riddle until you ask them to. Then follow these steps:

Use Picture Clues

- Ask a volunteer to identify the type of food shown on the plate. *(candy)*

- Point out the two hands in the picture and ask what each is doing. *(reaching for candy; saying "No!")*

Use Text Clues

- Read the first two sentences and invite children to speculate about the type of doctor this might be.

- Read the third sentence; encourage speculation about the type of doctor who has a special chair.

- Read the last two sentences.

I can be a man or a woman. I am a kind of doctor.

When you visit me, you sit in a special chair.

I tell you not to eat too much candy. If you have a toothache, I can help you.

Who Am I?

Answer the Riddle and Discuss Dentists

Invite volunteers to identify the worker *(a dentist)* and to talk about their experiences with the dentist.

Build Vocabulary and Concepts

- Guide children in comparing dentists and physicians and the work they do. Record comments in two columns, then reorganize them into a Venn diagram as shown below.

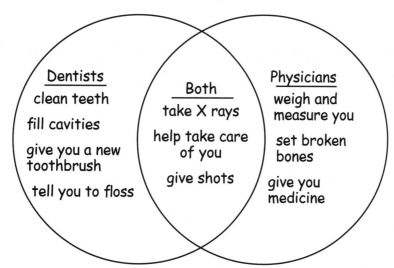

Dentists
clean teeth
fill cavities
give you a new toothbrush
tell you to floss

Both
take X rays
help take care of you
give shots

Physicians
weigh and measure you
set broken bones
give you medicine

- For independent practice, have students complete page 33.

8

I can be a man or a woman. I am a kind of doctor.

When you visit me, you sit in a special chair.

I tell you not to eat too much candy. If you have a toothache, I can help you.

Who Am I?

Clues to Comprehension, Grades 1–2 • EMC 2720

Open Wide!

1 Which one <u>cannot</u> be a **dentist**?

a doctor a man a vet a woman

2 Circle the word that rhymes with **tooth**.

boo booth both broth

3 Which word does <u>not</u> belong?

cast cavity drill filling

4 Which word is a synonym for **ache**?

ask ear ouch pain

5 In Box 1, draw foods that are <u>not</u> good for your teeth. In Box 2, draw foods that are good for your teeth. Add labels that name each food.

1	2

Present the Riddle: Workers

Remind children that the answer to this riddle is the name of a type of worker, and that they should not give the solution to the riddle until you ask them to. Then follow these steps:

Use Picture Clues

- Ask a volunteer to identify the object flying through the air. *(an airplane)*

- Invite volunteers to list who might be on the airplane. *(passengers, flight attendants, pilot, co-pilot)*

Use Text Clues

- Read the first sentence and ask children which of the people on the plane might wear a uniform. *(flight attendants, pilot and co-pilot, passengers in military uniform)*

- Read the rest of the text aloud, then ask a volunteer to point out the text that gives the strongest clue about who this worker is. Encourage children to say why they think that clue is the strongest. *(Answers may vary.)*

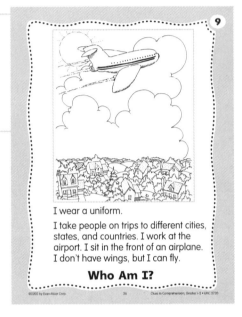

I wear a uniform.
I take people on trips to different cities, states, and countries. I work at the airport. I sit in the front of an airplane. I don't have wings, but I can fly.

Who Am I?

Answer the Riddle and Discuss Pilots

Invite volunteers to identify the worker *(a pilot)* and to share information they have about pilots, their training, and the work they do.

Build Vocabulary and Concepts

- Lead children in brainstorming information about pilots. Record information in a graphic organizer as shown below.

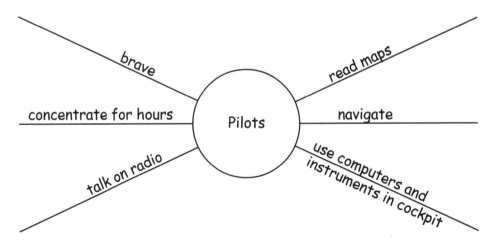

- For independent practice, have students complete page 36.

9

Present the Riddle: Workers

Remind children that the answer to this riddle is the name of a type of worker, and that they should not give the solution to the riddle until you ask them to. Then follow these steps:

Use Picture Clues

Invite volunteers to identify the items sitting on the table. *(an envelope and a letter)*

Use Text Clues

- Read the first two sentences and ask children if they have enough information to speculate about who this worker is. *(probably not)*

- Read the third sentence and reevaluate conjectures made previously.

- Read the last two sentences. Ask a volunteer to point out the text that gives the most information about this worker. *(I deliver letters.)*

I can be a man or a woman. I wear a uniform.
I visit your home each day except Sunday.
Sometimes I walk to your house; sometimes I drive my special truck. I deliver letters, postcards, and packages to you.

Who Am I?

Answer the Riddle and Discuss Mail Carriers

Invite volunteers to identify the worker *(a mail carrier)* and to share what they know about mail carriers and the work they do.

Build Vocabulary and Concepts

- Lead children in brainstorming the positive aspects and the negative aspects of a mail carrier's job. Record the ideas in a T-chart as shown below.

MAIL CARRIERS	
+ Positive Things	**–** Negative Things
make people happy get lots of exercise meet lots of people	get wet and cold in bad weather have to carry heavy things get barked at and bitten by dogs

- For independent practice, have students complete page 39.

10

I can be a man or a woman. I wear a uniform.

I visit your home each day except Sunday.

Sometimes I walk to your house; sometimes I drive my special truck. I deliver letters, postcards, and packages to you.

Who Am I?

Special Delivery

1 Complete this rhyme about mail carriers:

Neither rain nor snow nor sleet nor hail

will stop them from delivering _____.

2 Circle the word that sounds just like **mail**.

male   mall   pail   pale

3 Which word does <u>not</u> belong?

letter   package   postcard   truck

4 Which word is a synonym for **deliver**?

believer   bring   keep   liver

5 What is your favorite thing that a mail carrier brings you? On the back of this page, draw a picture of it, then write about what it is.

_____

_____

_____

_____

Who Am I?
A Firefighter

Present the Riddle: Workers

Remind children that the answer to this riddle is the name of a type of worker, and that they should not give the solution to the riddle until you ask them to. Then follow these steps:

Use Picture Clues

- Ask volunteers to describe what they see in the picture. *(a spotted dog sliding down a pole through the ceiling, helmets, boots, a city outside)*

- Invite children to say what kind of dog this is. *(a dalmatian, a fire dog)*

- Have children guess what kind of place this is. *(a fire station)*

Use Text Clues

- Read the first sentence and invite children to mention the community helpers they know about. Record them in a list. *(police officer, mail carrier, firefighter, sanitation workers, others as appropriate)*

- Read the next two sentences and work with children to cross off the list any workers who do not meet the new criteria.

- Read the last sentence.

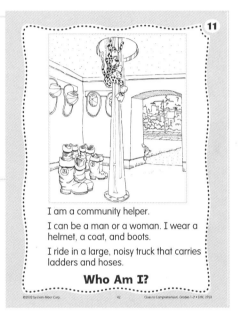

I am a community helper.

I can be a man or a woman. I wear a helmet, a coat, and boots.

I ride in a large, noisy truck that carries ladders and hoses.

Who Am I?

Answer the Riddle and Discuss Firefighters

Invite volunteers to identify the worker *(a firefighter)* and to share what they know about firefighters and the work they do.

Build Vocabulary and Concepts

- Choose three community workers from your list (including firefighters) and guide children in brainstorming descriptions of each; record ideas in separate lists. Then help children reorganize the information in a three-part Venn diagram as shown at right.

- For independent practice, have students complete page 42.

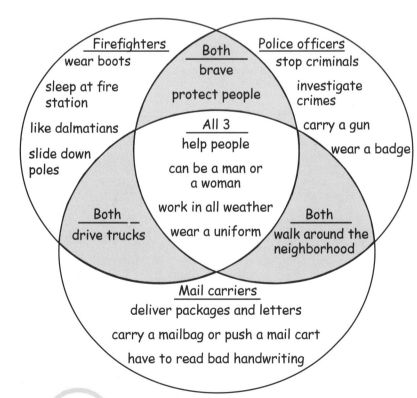

11

Present the Riddle: Workers

Remind children that the answer to this riddle is the name of a type of worker, and that they should not give the solution to the riddle until you ask them to. Then follow these steps:

Use Picture Clues

- Ask volunteers to describe the setting *(a carnival or circus)* and to identify the elements in the picture that helped them reach that conclusion. *(tent, ticket booth, circus car/cage, ringmaster)*

- Invite children to name some of the workers found at a circus.

Use Text Clues

- Have volunteers read the text in the speech bubble and on the ticket booth. *("Come one, come all!"; "Tickets")* Ask whether this information supports the conclusions already reached.

- Read the first two sentences and note that this text confirms that the setting is a circus.

- Read the last three sentences and ask children to make a mental picture of the worker described in the riddle.

I can be a man or a woman. I work in a circus.

People think I am funny. I wear a costume, wig, and makeup. My nose is big and red.

Who Am I?

Answer the Riddle and Discuss Clowns

Invite volunteers to identify the worker *(a clown)* and to describe the mental pictures they made. Have children share what they know about clowns and circus workers.

Build Vocabulary and Concepts

- Guide children in thinking about the positive and negative aspects of working as a clown. Record their comments in a T-chart as shown below.

CLOWNS	
+ Positive Things	**—** Negative Things
get to act silly all the time	have to act silly even if they're feeling bad
make people laugh	always traveling; don't get to stay home
travel around a lot	have to do dangerous tricks
get to work with animals	have to practice all the time
do lots of tricks and acrobatics	

- For independent practice, have students complete page 45.

12

I can be a man or a woman. I work in a circus.

People think I am funny. I wear a costume, wig, and makeup. My nose is big and red.

Who Am I?

ne:

Clowning Around

1 Complete this rhyme:

My nose is red and so is my wig.

My face is white; my shoes are big.

I make you laugh when I'm in town.

That's because I am a _____.

2 Circle the word that does <u>not</u> rhyme with **funny**.

bunny   fun   honey   money

3 Which word does <u>not</u> belong?

costume   engine   makeup   wig

4 Which word means the opposite of **funny**?

fun   silly   serious   sunny

5 If you were a clown, how would you dress? What would your makeup and hair be like? On the back of this page, draw a picture to show how you would look. Then write about some of the tricks you would do.

_____

_____

_____

45   Clues to Comprehension, Grades 1–2 • EMC 2720

Present the Riddle: Make-Believe Characters

Remind children that the answer to this riddle is the name of a character that some people think is make-believe, and that they should not give the solution to the riddle until you ask them to. Then follow these steps:

Use Picture Clues

- Invite volunteers to name the items they see in the picture. *(a present, a cat, a mouse, a Christmas tree with decorations)*

- Ask children what time of year they think it is in this picture, and how they can tell.

Use Text Clues

- Read the first two sentences and encourage children to speculate about who this person could be.

- Read the last three sentences.

Answer the Riddle and Discuss Santa Claus

Invite volunteers to identify this character *(Santa Claus)* and share what they know about him. Some children may think that Santa Claus is <u>not</u> a make-believe character. Use this opportunity to talk to children about respecting each others' right to hold individual opinions, especially during group discussions.

Build Vocabulary and Concepts

- Lead children in a brainstorming activity about Santa Claus. Record information about his various names, his appearance, and his activities in a graphic organizer as shown at right.

- For independent practice, have students complete page 48.

I am a chubby man. I have white hair. I wear a red suit. I'm very busy on December 24th. Children love the gifts I leave them.

Who Am I?

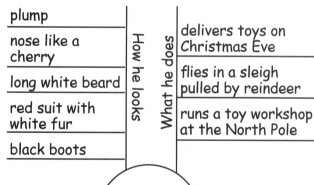

How he looks
- plump
- nose like a cherry
- long white beard
- red suit with white fur
- black boots

What he does
- delivers toys on Christmas Eve
- flies in a sleigh pulled by reindeer
- runs a toy workshop at the North Pole

SANTA CLAUS

Other names
- Santa
- St. Nick
- Kris Kringle

13

Where Am I?

1

I am outdoors. There are trees around me.

I stay in a tent here.

I roast marshmallows over the fire.
I sleep in my sleeping bag.

Where Am I?

©2002 by Evan-Moor Corp.

2

I am indoors. I need to buy a ticket to get inside this place. There are many seats here.

It is very dark inside.

I eat my popcorn while I watch a moving picture show.

Where Am I?

©2002 by Evan-Moor Corp.

3

I am indoors. There are machines in this place.

People bring baskets of dirty clothes here. They put coins in the machines.
People leave with clean clothes.

Where Am I?

©2002 by Evan-Moor Corp.

Present the Riddle: Places

Remind children that the answer to this riddle is a place, and that they should not give the solution to the riddle until you ask them to. Then follow these steps:

Use Picture Clues

- Ask volunteers to name the animals in the picture. *(bear, raccoon)*

- Have children name things that are part of nature (not made by humans). *(Moon, stars, wood, fire)*

- Invite children to tell about other things they see and to speculate about what this setting might be. *(marshmallow, skewer, person's hand; outdoors, campfire)*

Use Text Clues

- Read the first two sentences aloud and invite volunteers to point out words that confirm the setting. *(outdoors, trees)*

- Read the third sentence and ask volunteers to explain when and where people stay in tents. *(outdoors, camping, in emergencies)*

- Read the last two sentences.

I am outdoors. There are trees around me.

I stay in a tent here.

I roast marshmallows over the fire. I sleep in my sleeping bag.

Where Am I?

Answer the Riddle and Discuss Camping

Invite volunteers to identify the location *(a campground in a forest)*, and to share any camping experiences they have had.

Build Vocabulary and Concepts

- Work with children to create a packing list of items to bring on a camping trip. Include headings for categories such as *clothing, toiletries, camping gear*, and any others that children suggest.

- For independent practice, have students complete page 52.

CAMPING LIST		
Clothing	**Toiletries**	**Camping Gear**
jeans	toothbrush	flashlight
jacket	brush & comb	sleeping bag
T-shirts	washcloth	plate, cup, silverware
socks, underwear	toothpaste	tent
swimsuit	soap	air mattress
hiking boots	mosquito repellent	water bottle
pajamas	sunscreen	compass
hat	dental floss	

1

A Movie Theater

Present the Riddle: Places

Remind children that the answer to this riddle is a place, and that they should not give the solution to the riddle until you ask them to. Then follow these steps:

Use Picture Clues

- Ask volunteers to describe what they see in the picture. *(a tub of popcorn, a ticket stub, someone sitting in a theater seat)*

- Invite children to name some of the places where you might need a ticket to get in, and could sit and eat popcorn. *(a ballgame, a circus, a movie theater)*

Use Text Clues

- Read the first three sentences and ask children if this helps them to change or add to the list of possible places generated with picture clues.

- Read the fourth sentence and invite children to revise their list. *(Sporting events might be eliminated with this clue.)*

- Read the last sentence and make sure children know what a moving picture show is. *(another way to say "movies")*

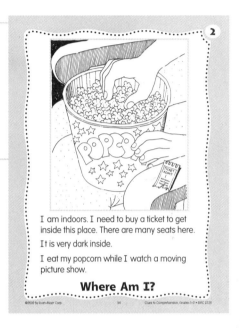

I am indoors. I need to buy a ticket to get inside this place. There are many seats here.
It is very dark inside.
I eat my popcorn while I watch a moving picture show.

Where Am I?

Answer the Riddle and Discuss Movie Theaters

Invite volunteers to identify the location *(a movie theater)*, and to share any experiences they have had at the movies.

Build Vocabulary and Concepts

- Choose three of the settings mentioned by children during analysis of picture clues (including the movie theater) and guide children in brainstorming features of each. Record ideas in separate lists. Then help children reorganize the information in a three-part Venn diagram as shown at right.

- For independent practice, have students complete page 55.

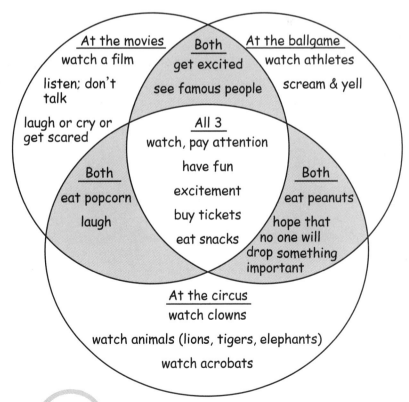

At the movies
watch a film
listen; don't talk
laugh or cry or get scared

Both
get excited
see famous people

At the ballgame
watch athletes
scream & yell

All 3
watch, pay attention
have fun
excitement
buy tickets
eat snacks

Both
eat popcorn
laugh

Both
eat peanuts
hope that no one will drop something important

At the circus
watch clowns
watch animals (lions, tigers, elephants)
watch acrobats

2

I am indoors. I need to buy a ticket to get inside this place. There are many seats here.

It is very dark inside.

I eat my popcorn while I watch a moving picture show.

Where Am I?

Lights Out!

1 Choose the best words to complete this sentence:

Movie theaters, ballparks, and circus tents are all places for

_____ .

eating fancy food	sitting outside
sitting in the dark	enjoying good entertainment

2 How many other words can you write that rhyme with **dark**?

_____

_____

3 Circle the word that does <u>not</u> belong.

movie   opera   parade   puppet show

4 Circle the word or words that are <u>not</u> a synonym for **movies**.

film   moving picture show   concert   theater

5 Imagine that you are at the movies. On the back of this page, draw a picture of what you see on the screen. Then write some sentences that tell what the movie is about.

_____

_____

A Laundromat

Present the Riddle: Places

Remind children that the answer to this riddle is a place, and that they should not give the solution to the riddle until you ask them to. Then follow these steps:

Use Picture Clues

- Ask volunteers to name what they see in the picture.
  (a girl, clothing, soap, a scrub brush)

- Have children describe what the girl is doing.
  (washing clothing, wringing out the water, scrubbing)

- Invite children to speculate about whether or not the girl is at home and, if not, where else she might be.

Use Text Clues

- Read the first two sentences and ask children whether they think the girl is at home.

- Read the next two sentences and invite children to revise their hypotheses. If they revise their hypotheses, ask them to explain their thinking.

- Read the last sentence.

I am indoors. There are machines in this place.

People bring baskets of dirty clothes here. They put coins in the machines.

People leave with clean clothes.

Where Am I?

©2002 by Evan-Moor Corp.   58   Clues to Comprehension, Grades 1-2 • EMC 2720

Answer the Riddle and Discuss Laundromats

Invite volunteers to identify the location *(a laundromat)*, and to share any experiences they have had at laundromats. You may wish to comment that even people who have washing machines and dryers at home may use laundromats when traveling away from home.

Build Vocabulary and Concepts

- Discuss how people cleaned their clothing before washers, dryers, and laundromats were invented. Discuss the advantages and disadvantages of hand-washing and air-drying as compared to machine-washing and drying. Record comments in a comparison chart as shown below.

	Cost	Use of energy	Use of time	Result
hand-washing	just need to buy soap & water	uses human energy	takes lots of time	clothes get worn out from scrubbing
machine-washing	have to buy a washing machine or pay to use one	uses electricity; uses water	you can do other things while the machine washes	clothes get clean
air-drying	free	uses energy from the sun	you can do other things while the clothes dry	clothes smell good, but they feel stiff
machine-drying	have to buy a dryer or pay to use one	uses electricity or gas	you can do other things while the clothes dry	clothes are warm and soft

- For independent practice, have students complete page 58.

3

The Airport

Present the Riddle: Places

Remind children that the answer to this riddle is a place, and that they should not give the solution to the riddle until you ask them to. Then follow these steps:

Use Picture Clues

- Ask a volunteer to point to the window in the picture, and to say what can be seen through the window. *(airplanes)*

- Have another child describe what is happening indoors. *(Someone is pushing a luggage cart with suitcases and travelers.)*

Use Text Clues

- Invite volunteers to point to any text in the picture that could help provide clues about this setting. *("tickets," "New York" and "California" stickers on luggage; baggage routing ticket)*

- Read the first three sentences and invite volunteers to say whether this information adds anything to what is already known.

- Read the last two sentences and check again to see if this has added any new information.

I am inside a very large building. It is very busy here. There are many people inside.

They are carrying suitcases and tickets.

I see airplanes outside.

Where Am I?

Answer the Riddle and Discuss Airports

Invite volunteers to identify the location *(the airport)*, and to share any experiences they have had at airports, traveling or picking up or dropping off travelers.

Build Vocabulary and Concepts

- Remind children that airports are busy places because travelers are always coming and going. Point out that many people also work at airports. Guide children in a brainstorming activity about vehicles, workers, and jobs at airports. Record their comments on a graphic organizer as shown at right.

- For independent practice, have students complete page 61.

AIRPORTS		
Vehicles	**Workers**	**Jobs**
airplanes	pilots	flying planes
helicopters	flight attendants	carrying luggage
jets	security people	keeping people safe
trailers	luggage handlers	selling things
motorcycles	salespeople in stores	making and serving food
buses	shoeshine people	helping people buy tickets
limos	food servers	
	ticket sellers	

4

I am inside a very large building. It is very busy here. There are many people inside.

They are carrying suitcases and tickets. I see airplanes outside.

Where Am I?

Away We Go!

1 Which one would <u>not</u> be found at an **airport**?

airplanes   suitcases   tickets   train tracks

2 How many other words can you write that rhyme with **plane** and **train**?

_____

_____

3 Circle the word that is the opposite of **busy**.

bus   calm   dizzy   wild

4 Circle the word that sounds like **plane**.

pan   pain   plain   plan

5 Imagine that you could work at an airport. Which job would you choose? On the back of this page, draw a picture of yourself doing that job. Then write about what you do.

_____

_____

_____

_____

Present the Riddle: Places

Remind children that the answer to this riddle is a place, and that they should not give the solution to the riddle until you ask them to. Then follow these steps:

Use Picture Clues

- Ask a volunteer to say what is fluttering through the air in this picture. *(confetti)*

- Have children say what else they see in this scene *(a boy squatting down, a dog, a cat, people's legs)* and to speculate about why the boy is crouching down. *(to see through the crowd)*

- Invite children to tell how the boy and the animals might be feeling, and how they can tell. *(happy, excited; by the expressions on their faces)*

Use Text Clues

- Read the first two sentences and ask children if the person speaking is the boy shown in the picture, and how they know. *(No. He is not standing.)*

- Read the last three sentences and invite volunteers to point to the text that they think gives the best clues about this scene. *(Answers will vary..)*

I am outdoors. I am standing on the sidewalk.

I see people waving flags. People playing instruments are marching down the street. Some people are driving decorated cars.

Where Am I?

Answer the Riddle and Discuss Parades

Invite volunteers to identify the location *(at a parade)*, and to share any experiences they have had at parades, the types of parades they have seen or participated in, and how they have felt in large crowds.

Build Vocabulary and Concepts

- Guide students in brainstorming about the sights, sounds, and smells at a parade. Record their comments on a graphic organizer as shown at right.

- For independent practice, have students complete page 64.

PARADES		
What you see	What you hear	What you smell
stilt-walkers	music	fireworks smoke
dragon-dancers	firecrackers	food
Uncle Sam	laughing	exhaust from trucks with floats
clowns	noise	
bands		

5

Where Am I?
The Zoo

Present the Riddle: Places
Remind children that the answer to this riddle is a place, and that they should not give the solution to the riddle until you ask them to. Then follow these steps:

Use Picture Clues
- Ask a volunteer to name the animals—or parts of animals— that they see in this picture. *(mice, elephant's trunk and foot)*
- Have children name the other things they see. *(a fence, a bag of peanuts, a sign)*

Use Text Clues
- Have a volunteer read the sign in the picture. Then read the first three sentences and have children speculate about where the peanuts in the picture came from.
- Read the last two sentences and invite volunteers to point to the text that they think gives the best clues about this place. *(Answers will vary..)*

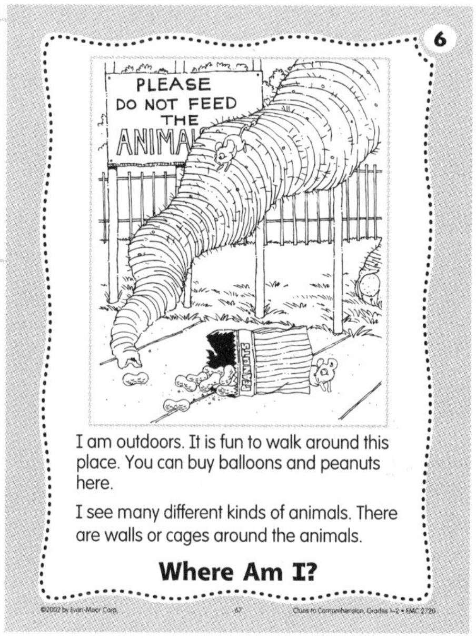

Answer the Riddle and Discuss Zoos
Invite volunteers to identify the location *(a zoo)*, and to share any experiences they have had at a zoo or wild animal park.

Build Vocabulary and Concepts
- Guide children in discussing the difference between animals that live in the wild and those that live in captivity in a zoo. Record their comments on a graphic organizer as shown below. Afterward, encourage children to take and defend a position about which environment is better for animals. Help children use logical arguments.
- For independent practice, have students complete page 67.

PLEASE DO NOT FEED THE ANIMALS

I am outdoors. It is fun to walk around this place. You can buy balloons and peanuts here.

I see many different kinds of animals. There are walls or cages around the animals.

Where Am I?

WILD ANIMALS	
In the wild	**In a zoo**
live free, in the open	live locked in a cage
have to feed and care for themselves	taken care of by people
can be killed by hunters or predators	protected from being hurt
hard for people to see them	easy for people to see them

6

I am outdoors. It is fun to walk around this place. You can buy balloons and peanuts here.

I see many different kinds of animals. There are walls or cages around the animals.

Where Am I?

A Wild Time

1 Circle the sentence that is <u>not</u> true.

Zoos help protect animals.   Zoos help people enjoy animals.

You can see dinosaurs at a zoo.   Some animals at zoos are not in cages.

2 How many other words can you write that rhyme with **zoo**?

_____

_____

3 Circle the word that means the opposite of **wild**.

fierce   tame   while   will

4 Which animal is <u>not</u> found at a **zoo**?

elephant   lion   shark   tiger

5 Which animal would you like to see at the zoo? On the back of this page, draw a picture of it, then write about why you like it.

_____

_____

_____

_____

Present the Riddle: Places

Remind children that the answer to this riddle is a place, and that they should not give the solution to the riddle until you ask them to. Then follow these steps:

Use Picture Clues

- Invite a volunteer to describe what can be seen through the window in the picture. *(a girl hanging upside down on the bars with a book)*

- Have another child name the things that can be seen inside. *(books, an aquarium)*

Use Text Clues

- Ask a volunteer to read the words on the books in the picture. Ask where you usually see that kind of book. *(at school)*

- Read the first two sentences and invite volunteers to speculate about what sort of place this might be.

- Read the last three sentences and ask children to point out the words that give the best clues about this location. *(Answers will vary..)*

I am inside a building. There are many rooms here.

I see yellow buses parked outside. Children study here. A teacher helps them learn.

Where Am I?

Answer the Riddle and Discuss Schools

Invite volunteers to identify the location *(a school)*, and to compare their school experiences with those described in the text of the riddle or pictured in the illustration.

Build Vocabulary and Concepts

- Ask children to name things that <u>all</u> schools have; record them in a list. Then have them name things that some schools have, but that other schools might not. Note these items in another list. Then model how to record this information in a graphic organizer that shows information about "some schools" as a subset of the larger group, "all schools."

- For independent practice, have students complete page 70.

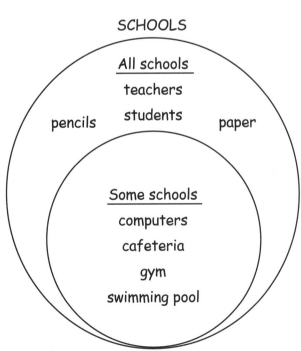

SCHOOLS

<u>All schools</u>
teachers
pencils   students   paper

<u>Some schools</u>
computers
cafeteria
gym
swimming pool

7

Where Am I?
A Park

Present the Riddle: Places

Remind children that the answer to this riddle is a place, and that they should not give the solution to the riddle until you ask them to. Then follow these steps:

Use Picture Clues

- Invite a volunteer to name the living things in the picture.
  (boy, dog, bird, frog)

- Ask another child to name the nonliving things that can be seen.
  (a fountain, a bench, a basketball)

- Encourage children to speculate about the setting of this scene.

Use Text Clues

- Read the first two sentences and ask children if they provide any new information to help them revise their hypotheses.

- Read the last three sentences and ask children to point out the words that give the best clues about this location.
  (Answers will vary.)

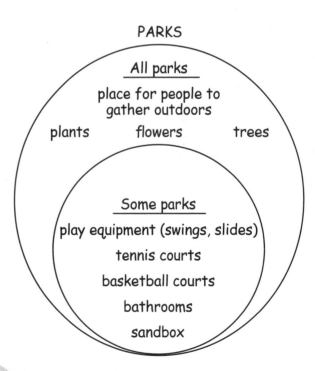

I am outdoors. I see trees, grass, and benches.

There are lots of children. They come here to play. I see a slide and swings.

Where Am I?

©2002 by Evan-Moor Corp.   73   Clues to Comprehension, Grades 1–2 • EMC 2720

Answer the Riddle and Discuss Parks

Invite volunteers to identify the location *(a park)*, and to talk about neighborhood and city parks where they play.

Build Vocabulary and Concepts

- As children share information about familiar parks, record the features they name. Then work with children to identify which features are common to all parks, and which occur only in some parks. Record this information in a graphic organizer that shows information about "some parks" as a subset of the larger group, "all parks."

- For independent practice, have students complete page 73.

PARKS

All parks

place for people to gather outdoors

plants   flowers   trees

Some parks

play equipment (swings, slides)

tennis courts

basketball courts

bathrooms

sandbox

8

I am outdoors. I see trees, grass, and benches.

There are lots of children. They come here to play. I see a slide and swings.

Where Am I?

Play Time

1 Circle a place that would <u>not</u> have a **park**.

a campground   a children's center   a fancy restaurant   a school

2 How many other words can you write that rhyme with **play**?

_____

_____

3 Which words are <u>not</u> synonyms for **play**?

fool around   have fun   have a good time   make trouble

4 Circle the word that does <u>not</u> belong.

monkey bars   jungle   slide   swings

5 What would the perfect park look like? On the back of this page, draw a picture of it and write a short description.

_____

_____

_____

_____

Present the Riddle: Places

Remind children that the answer to this riddle is a place, and that they should not give the solution to the riddle until you ask them to. Then follow these steps:

Use Picture Clues

- Ask a volunteer to describe what is happening in this picture. *(A man is trying to stay cool in the hot sun.)*

- Invite children to point out the things that help them know that it is very hot in this picture. *(The man is sweating. Cold liquid in the pitcher and hot sun are creating condensation on the pitcher and glass. The man has on sunglasses and a hat, and is trying to find shade under an umbrella. The man is dressed for hot weather.)*

- Ask children if they see any water here, like a beach or lake. *(No.)*

Use Text Clues

- Invite a volunteer to read the title of the book being read by the man.

- Read the first two sentences and encourage children to speculate about where this man is.

- Read the last three sentences and ask children to point out the words that give the best clues about this location. *(Answers will vary..)*

I am outdoors. It is very sunny and hot during the day in this place.

It is very dry here because it does not rain a lot. I see a lot of sand and rocks. There are cactus plants all around.

Where Am I?

Answer the Riddle and Discuss Deserts

Invite volunteers to identify the location *(a desert)*, and to share what they know about deserts. Point out that the man in this picture is not appropriately dressed for the desert at all, because it is important to protect skin from the hot desert sun.

Build Vocabulary and Concepts

- Guide children in brainstorming about the features of a desert. *(what it looks like, the sorts of plants and animals that live there)* Organize information on an attribute chart as shown at right.

- For independent practice, have students complete page 76.

Look like this	Don't look like this
sand	green
rocks	river, lake, stream
no water	grass, trees
brown	wet, rainy
dry	

DESERTS

Plants & animals that live there	Plants & animals that don't live there
cactus	tall trees
lizards	polar bears
snakes	
tortoises	

9

Where Am I?
A Bakery

Present the Riddle: Places

Remind children that the answer to this riddle is a place, and that they should not give the solution to the riddle until you ask them to. Then follow these steps:

Use Picture Clues

- Ask a volunteer to say what the man in the picture is holding. *(a pie)*

- Ask what the man has on his head and why he is wearing it. *(a hat; to keep his hair out of the food when he works)*

- Invite volunteers to speculate about where this man works.

Use Text Clues

- Ask a volunteer to read the words on the man's hat. Invite volunteers to explain what "wares" are. *(something that you offer for sale)*

- Read the first two sentences and ask children how they think the pie smells.

- Read the next two sentences and ask children to speculate about the kinds of foods sold in this place.

- Read the last sentence and note whether children's hypotheses were correct.

I am in a kind of shop. When I walk in, it smells delicious!

Food is baked in ovens here. They put the food in glass cases so I can see it.

I can buy fresh bread, doughnuts, and sweet desserts here.

Where Am I?

Answer the Riddle and Discuss Bakeries

Invite volunteers to identify the location *(a bakery)*, and to share what they know about bakeries.

Build Vocabulary and Concepts

- Guide children in brainstorming about the sights and smells of a bakery. Record information on a graphic organizer as shown at right.

- For independent practice, have students complete page 79.

BAKERIES		
What they sell	**How they smell**	**What you see there**
bread	delicious	bakers in white hats and aprons
pastries	like fresh bread	racks of bread and goodies cooling
cookies	sweet	ovens
cakes	like coffee	glass cases with baked things
doughnuts		

I am in a kind of shop. When I walk in, it smells delicious!

Food is baked in ovens here. They put the food in glass cases so I can see it.

I can buy fresh bread, doughnuts, and sweet desserts here.

Where Am I?

ne:

Hot Cross Buns

1 Choose the words that <u>cannot</u> complete this sentence:

Almost everything in a bakery is made _____.

| by a baker | in the oven | of vegetables | to sell to people |

2 How many other words can you write that rhyme with **bake**?

_____

_____

3 Which word is an antonym for **sweet**?

     cold   hot   sour   sugary

4 Circle the word that does <u>not</u> belong.

     cake   doughnut   pie   steak

5 What is your favorite thing to buy at a bakery? On the back of this page, draw a picture of it. Then describe it in writing.

_____

_____

_____

_____

A Grocery Store

Present the Riddle: Places

Remind children that the answer to this riddle is a place, and that they should not give the solution to the riddle until you ask them to. Then follow these steps:

Use Picture Clues

- Ask a volunteer to tell what the dogs are looking at.
  (a shopping cart)

- Invite volunteers to speculate about what kind of store this is.

Use Text Clues

- Ask volunteers to read the words or numbers on the window signs.

- Read the first two sentences aloud. Ask children to speculate about the kind of store this might be.

- Read the rest of the riddle and have children point out the words they think are most helpful in giving clues about the kind of store this might be.

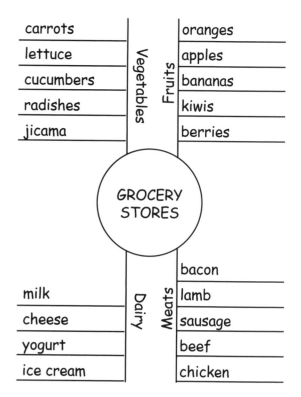

I am in a building. It is a kind of store. There are many shelves here. I push my cart down the long aisles. I can buy all kinds of food here.

Where Am I?

Answer the Riddle and Discuss Grocery Stores

Invite volunteers to identify the location *(a grocery store)*, and to share what they know about grocery stores.

Build Vocabulary and Concepts

- Guide children in brainstorming about the items found in grocery stores. Organize them by category on a graphic organizer as shown at right.

- For independent practice, have students complete page 82.

Vegetables	Fruits
carrots	oranges
lettuce	apples
cucumbers	bananas
radishes	kiwis
jicama	berries

GROCERY STORES

Dairy	Meats
	bacon
milk	lamb
cheese	sausage
yogurt	beef
ice cream	chicken

11

The Beach

Present the Riddle: Places

Remind children that the answer to this riddle is a place, and that they should not give the solution to the riddle until you ask them to. Then follow these steps:

Use Picture Clues

- Ask a volunteer to name the animals in the picture. *(a seagull and a crab)*

- Invite a volunteer to name the toys in the picture. *(shovels, pails, molds for shaping sand)*

- Encourage children to say what has been happening in this scene. *(someone has been making a sand castle)*

Use Text Clues

- Read the first three sentences aloud and encourage children to speculate about where this might be.

- Read the last two sentences and have children say whether this confirms their hypotheses.

Answer the Riddle and Discuss the Beach

Invite volunteers to identify the location *(the beach)*, and to share what they know about beaches.

Build Vocabulary and Concepts

- Guide children in comparing the seashore with a lakeshore. Use a Venn diagram like the one below to organize their comments.

> I am outdoors. I see a lot of water. People are wearing swimsuits.
>
> Children are using shovels and pails to build castles. There are seashells on the sand.
>
> **Where Am I?**

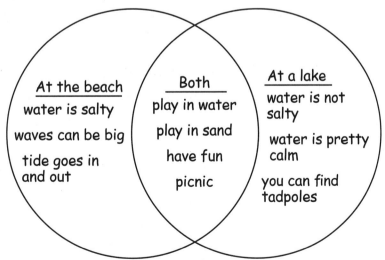

At the beach
water is salty
waves can be big
tide goes in and out

Both
play in water
play in sand
have fun
picnic

At a lake
water is not salty
water is pretty calm
you can find tadpoles

- For independent practice, have students complete page 85.

12

I am outdoors. I see a lot of water. People are wearing swimsuits.

Children are using shovels and pails to build castles. There are seashells on the sand.

Where Am I?

By the Seashore

1 Say this tongue twister aloud three times:

She sells seashells by the seashore.

2 How many other words can you write that rhyme with **shore**?

_____

_____

3 Which word is an antonym for **wet**?

cold   soggy   dry   went

4 Circle the word that does <u>not</u> belong.

freeway   gull   sand   water

5 What is your favorite thing to do at the beach? On the back of this page, draw a picture of yourself doing it, then write about what you are doing.

_____

_____

_____

_____

Present the Riddle: Places

Remind children that the answer to this riddle is a place, and that they should not give the solution to the riddle until you ask them to. Then follow these steps:

Use Picture Clues

- Ask a volunteer to name the object in the picture. *(a book)*

- Invite a volunteer to say what the make-believe creature in the picture is *(a bookworm)*, and to explain what a "bookworm" is. *(someone who loves books and reading)*

Use Text Clues

- Read the first two sentences aloud and invite children to speculate about what sort of building this is.

- Read the next two sentences and encourage students to revise their hypotheses.

- Read the last sentence. Then invite a volunteer to read the words spoken by the bookworm and to speculate about what sort of place would be a great home for a bookworm.

WOW, WHAT A GREAT HOME!

I am in a large building. There are many tables and chairs.

It is very quiet here. People are studying and reading.

I see many books on shelves.

Where Am I?

Answer the Riddle and Discuss Libraries

Invite volunteers to identify the location *(the library)*, and to share what they know about libraries. You may need to explain the difference between a library *(a place where you can borrow books)* and a bookstore *(a place where you can buy books)*.

Build Vocabulary and Concepts

- Guide children in a discussion about the library, the materials found there, and the rules for behavior in a library. Record their ideas in a graphic organizer as shown below.

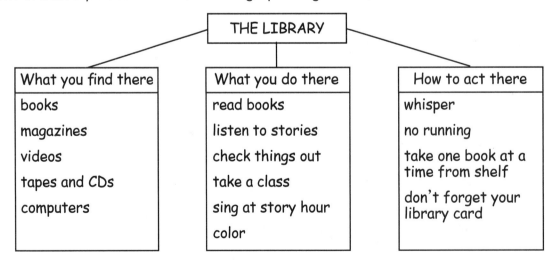

THE LIBRARY

What you find there	What you do there	How to act there
books	read books	whisper
magazines	listen to stories	no running
videos	check things out	take one book at a time from shelf
tapes and CDs	take a class	don't forget your library card
computers	sing at story hour	
	color	

- For independent practice, have students complete page 88.

13

Present the Riddle: Places

Remind children that the answer to this riddle is a place, and that they should not give the solution to the riddle until you ask them to. Then follow these steps:

Use Picture Clues

- Ask a volunteer to describe the scene in the picture. *(table, chairs, place settings)*

- Invite children to speculate about whether this scene is in a home, and what makes them think so.

Use Text Clues

- Invite a volunteer to read the words on the sign on the table. Ask children if this information makes them want to revise their hypotheses about the setting.

- Read the first two sentences and ask children if this information supports their hypotheses about this location.

- Read the last two sentences and invite volunteers to point out the text they feel is most helpful in giving clues about this location.

I am in a place that has many tables and chairs. There are forks, knives, and spoons on each table.

You can eat breakfast, lunch, or dinner here. A cook makes your food in the kitchen, and then someone brings the food to your table.

Where Am I?

Answer the Riddle and Discuss Restaurants

Invite volunteers to identify the location *(a restaurant)*, and to share what they know about restaurants.

Build Vocabulary and Concepts

- Guide children in comparing dining experiences in a restaurant and at home. Record their comments in a Venn diagram as shown at right.

- For independent practice, have students complete page 91.

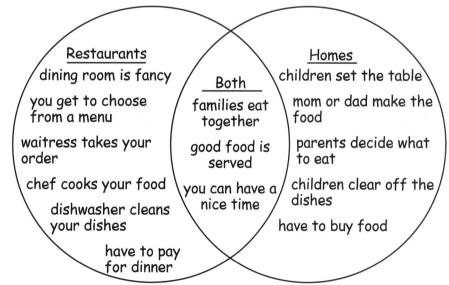

Restaurants
- dining room is fancy
- you get to choose from a menu
- waitress takes your order
- chef cooks your food
- dishwasher cleans your dishes
- have to pay for dinner

Both
- families eat together
- good food is served
- you can have a nice time

Homes
- children set the table
- mom or dad make the food
- parents decide what to eat
- children clear off the dishes
- have to buy food

I am in a place that has many tables and chairs. There are forks, knives, and spoons on each table.

You can eat breakfast, lunch, or dinner here. A cook makes your food in the kitchen, and then someone brings the food to your table.

Where Am I?

ne: _____

Eating Out

1 Choose the words that <u>cannot</u> complete this sentence:

At a restaurant, you _____.

can eat a meal or a snack	choose from many foods
can look in the refrigerator for food	pay for your meal

2 Circle the word that rhymes with **food**.

fool good mood wood

3 Which word is a synonym for **cook**?

banker chef cookie waiter

4 Circle the word that does <u>not</u> belong.

breakfast cake dinner lunch

5 What is your favorite dessert to order when you eat out? On the back of this page, draw a picture of it, then write a description of it.

_____

_____

_____

_____

What Am I?

I am a forest animal. I am black and white. I have a bushy tail.

When enemies come near, I give off a bad smell.

What Am I?

CHARLOTTE'S DINER
BUGS WELCOME!

I am a small creature. I crawl or swing through the air. I make my own special house.

I eat bugs that I catch in my house. I have eight legs.

What Am I?

...am a speedy animal with long ears. ...p using strong back legs. I can be wild or tame. I like to eat carrots.

What Am I?

Present the Riddle: Animals

Remind children that the answer to this riddle is an animal, and that they should not give the solution to the riddle until you ask them to. Then follow these steps:

Use Picture Clues

- Ask a volunteer to name the animals in the picture. *(raccoon, bear)*

- Have children describe the person in the picture, what he was probably doing just before the scene shown here *(hiking or hunting in the woods)*, and what they see in the picture to support their opinions. *(He is wearing a hunter's cap and carrying a backpack and bedroll.)*

- Invite a volunteer to describe what the man and animals are doing *(holding their noses and running away)*, and to speculate about the reason for their behavior. *(Something must smell awful.)*

Use Text Clues

- Read the first three sentences and invite children to speculate about what animal this might be.

- Read the last sentence and encourage children to speculate about what this animal might consider to be an "enemy."

I am a forest animal. I am black and white. I have a bushy tail.

When enemies come near, I give off a bad smell.

What Am I?

Answer the Riddle and Discuss Skunks

Invite volunteers to identify the animal *(a skunk)*, and to share what they know about skunks and any experiences with skunks that they may have had.

Build Vocabulary and Concepts

- Reread the riddle, then work with children to brainstorm synonyms for these words: *forest*, *bushy*, *bad*, and *smell*. Record their ideas on a graphic organizer as shown below.

Synonyms	
forest	woods, wilderness
bushy	furry, fuzzy
bad	icky, yucky, ugly, nasty, stinky
smell	odor, stink, aroma

- For independent practice, have students complete page 95.

1

I am a forest animal. I am black and white. I have a bushy tail.

When enemies come near, I give off a bad smell.

What Am I?

Hold Your Nose!

1 Choose the word that <u>cannot</u> complete this sentence:

A skunk is usually a _____ animal.

| forest | stinky | tame | wild |

2 How many other words can you write that rhyme with **smell**?

_____

_____

3 Which word means the opposite of **enemy**?

enormous   foe   friend   soldier

4 Circle the word that does <u>not</u> belong.

bear   deer   giraffe   skunk

5 What would you do if you saw a skunk in the forest? On the back of this page, draw a picture of what you would do. Then write about how you might feel if you saw a skunk.

_____

_____

_____

Present the Riddle: Animals

Remind children that the answer to this riddle is an animal, and that they should not give the solution to the riddle until you ask them to. Then follow these steps:

Use Picture Clues

- Invite children to look closely at the creatures in the picture, then ask a volunteer to describe the special characteristics of these creatures. *(They have 6 legs—or 4 legs and 2 arms. They have antennae. One has wings. They have big eyes.)*

Use Text Clues

- Ask a volunteer to read the words on the sign in the picture.

- Read the first three sentences and invite children to speculate about what sort of animal this might be.

- Read the last two sentences and ask children to study the picture again for any visual clues about the "house" made by this animal. *(a spider web)*

I am a small creature. I crawl or swing through the air. I make my own special house.

I eat bugs that I catch in my house. I have eight legs.

What Am I?

Answer the Riddle and Discuss Spiders

Invite volunteers to identify the animal *(a spider)*, and to share what they know about spiders. You may need to explain the humor in the sign in the picture by telling children that there is a famous children's book about a spider called *Charlotte's Web*. You may also wish to emphasize that spiders are not insects. *(Insects have three body parts and six legs; spiders have eight legs.)*

Build Vocabulary and Concepts

- Guide children in brainstorming what they know about insects and spiders. Record their comments in a Venn diagram as shown at right.

- For independent practice, have students complete page 98.

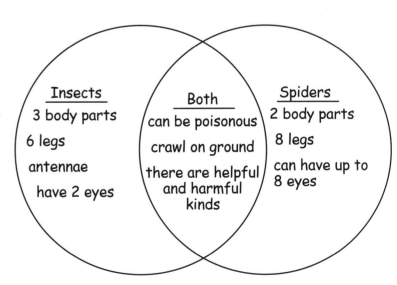

Insects
3 body parts
6 legs
antennae
have 2 eyes

Both
can be poisonous
crawl on ground
there are helpful and harmful kinds

Spiders
2 body parts
8 legs
can have up to 8 eyes

2

Present the Riddle: Animals

Remind children that the answer to this riddle is an animal, and that they should not give the solution to the riddle until you ask them to. Then follow these steps:

Use Picture Clues

- Ask volunteers to describe the setting. Is it the city, the countryside, the beach, the forest? *(the countryside, a farm)* Ask what clues in the picture help them support their answers. *(a barn with hay and a horse in it, vegetables planted in rows)*

Use Text Clues

- Ask a volunteer to read the words on the sign in the picture and to explain who "Mr. MacGregor" is. *(a farmer in the "Peter Rabbit" stories of Beatrix Potter)*

- Read the first sentence and encourage children to speculate about what sort of animal this might be.

- Read the second sentence and invite children to revise their hypotheses based on this new information.

- Read the last two sentences and ask volunteers to point out the words that provide the strongest clue about this animal.

I am a speedy animal with long ears.
I hop using strong back legs.
I can be wild or tame. I like to eat carrots.

What Am I?

Answer the Riddle and Discuss Rabbits

Invite volunteers to identify the animal *(a rabbit)*, and to share what they know about rabbits.

Build Vocabulary and Concepts

- Guide children in comparing wild and tame rabbits. Record their comments in a Venn diagram as shown at right.

- For independent practice, have students complete page 101.

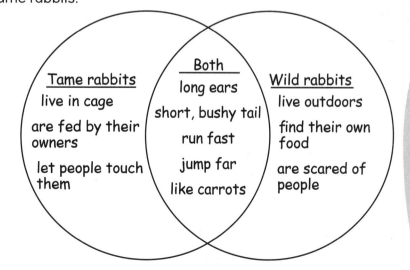

Tame rabbits
live in cage
are fed by their owners
let people touch them

Both
long ears
short, bushy tail
run fast
jump far
like carrots

Wild rabbits
live outdoors
find their own food
are scared of people

3

I am a speedy animal with long ears.

I hop using strong back legs.

I can be wild or tame. I like to eat carrots.

What Am I?

name:

Cotton Tail

1 Choose the words that <u>cannot</u> complete this sentence:

A rabbit can_____ in a garden.

cause problems   eat carrots   help plant seeds   hop around

2 How many other words can you write that rhyme with **hop**?

_____

_____

3 Which word means the opposite of **wild**?

crazy   curious   tame   wilder

4 Circle the word that does <u>not</u> belong.

beet   carrot   lemon   potato

5 Do you like wild rabbits or tame rabbits? On the back of this page, draw a picture of the kind of rabbit you prefer. Write some sentences that tell about it.

_____

_____

_____

Present the Riddle: Animals

Remind children that the answer to this riddle is an animal, and that they should not give the solution to the riddle until you ask them to. Then follow these steps:

Use Picture Clues

- Ask a volunteer to describe the picture. *(A cat and two kittens are staring hungrily at a bottle of milk.)*

Use Text Clues

- Ask a volunteer to read the word on the bottle in the picture.

- Read the first two sentences and encourage children to speculate about what sort of animal this might be.

- Read the last two sentences and invite children to revise their hypotheses based on this new information.

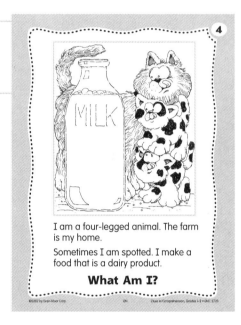

I am a four-legged animal. The farm is my home.

Sometimes I am spotted. I make a food that is a dairy product.

What Am I?

Answer the Riddle and Discuss Cows

Invite volunteers to identify the animal *(a cow)*, and to share what they know about cows.

Build Vocabulary and Concepts

- Guide children in brainstorming dairy products. Record their comments in a graphic organizer as shown below.

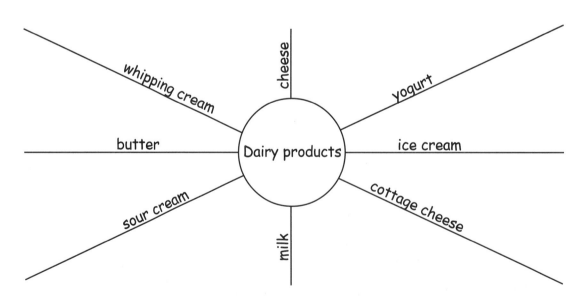

- For independent practice, have students complete page 104.

What Am I?
A Bird

Present the Riddle: Animals

Remind children that the answer to this riddle is an animal, and that they should not give the solution to the riddle until you ask them to. Then follow these steps:

Use Picture Clues

- Ask a volunteer to describe the picture. *(A feather is floating down onto a dog.)*

Use Text Clues

- Read the first sentence and encourage children to brainstorm a list of two-legged animals.

- Read the last two sentences and have children direct you in crossing off the list all entries that are eliminated with these clues.

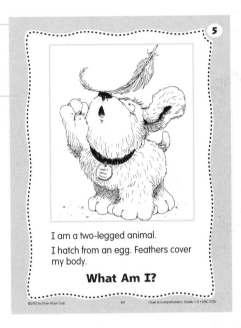

I am a two-legged animal.
I hatch from an egg. Feathers cover my body.

What Am I?

Answer the Riddle and Discuss Birds

Invite volunteers to identify the animal *(a bird)*, and to share what they know about birds.

Build Vocabulary and Concepts

- Refer back to the list of two-legged, feathered animals that hatch from eggs and use it in working with children to identify characteristics common to all birds as well as those specific to only some birds. Record comments in a graphic organizer as shown below.

- For independent practice, have students complete page 107.

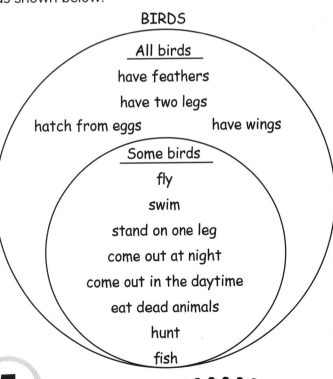

BIRDS

All birds

have feathers

have two legs

hatch from eggs   have wings

Some birds

fly

swim

stand on one leg

come out at night

come out in the daytime

eat dead animals

hunt

fish

5

I am a two-legged animal.

I hatch from an egg. Feathers cover my body.

What Am I?

Birds of a Feather

1 Choose the word or words that <u>cannot</u> complete this sentence:

Most birds _____.

| build nests | fly | lay eggs | swim |

2 Circle the words that rhyme with **bird**.

heard   beard   stirred   word

3 Which word is a synonym for **fly**?

drive   soar   try   walk

4 Circle the word that does <u>not</u> belong.

beak   feathers   snout   wing

5 On the back of this page, draw a picture of your favorite bird. Write some sentences to describe it.

_____

_____

_____

_____

What Am I?
A Kangaroo

Present the Riddle: Animals

Remind children that the answer to this riddle is an animal, and that they should not give the solution to the riddle until you ask them to. Then follow these steps:

Use Picture Clues

- Ask a volunteer to trace the dashed lines in the picture and to say what they represent. *(a jumping movement)*
- Invite children to describe the other things they see in the picture. *(a piece of land surrounded by water, fish)*

Use Text Clues

- Ask a volunteer to read the big word in the picture. If children are not familiar with Australia, explain that it is a continent—one of the huge masses of land that make up our Earth.
- Read the first two sentences and encourage children to speculate about what kind of animal this is.
- Read the last two sentences and invite children to revise their hypotheses based on the new information.

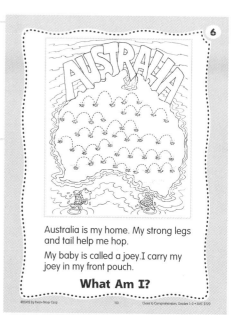

Australia is my home. My strong legs and tail help me hop.

My baby is called a joey. I carry my joey in my front pouch.

What Am I?

Answer the Riddle and Discuss Kangaroos

Invite volunteers to identify the animal *(a kangaroo)*, and to share what they know about kangaroos.

Build Vocabulary and Concepts

- Guide children in a brainstorm of facts about kangaroos. Record their comments in a graphic organizer as shown below.

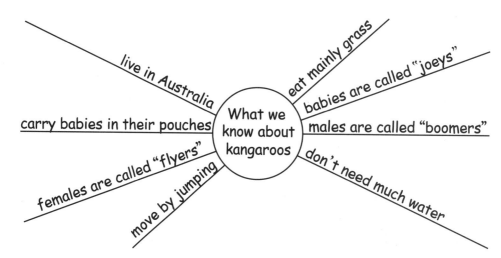

- For independent practice, have students complete page 110.

6

Present the Riddle: Things

Remind children that the answer to this riddle is a thing, and that they should not give the solution to the riddle until you ask them to. Then follow these steps:

Use Picture Clues

- Ask a volunteer to name the items shown in the picture. *(a fish in a tank, a dog, a piece of furniture, a hand with a string looped around one finger)*

- Invite children to speculate about what might be at the other end of the string.

Use Text Clues

- Read the first two sentences, and encourage children to speculate about what sort of toy this might be. Record ideas in a list.

- Read the last three sentences and invite children to revise their hypotheses based on the new information, crossing items off the list as you revise.

IS SOMETHING MISSING?

I am round. I am a toy.
You hold me in your hand. I have a long string. I go down and up.

What Am I?

©2002 by Evan-Moor Corp.   113   Clues to Comprehension, Grades 1-2 • EMC 2720

Answer the Riddle and Discuss Yo-Yos

Invite volunteers to identify the item *(a yo-yo)*, and to share what they know about yo-yos.

Build Vocabulary and Concepts

- Refer to the list of toys begun when children used picture clues. Lead children in brainstorming other round toys. Then have children help you sort the list, recording the names of all round toys that are balls as a subset of the larger category, "All round toys," as shown at right.

- For independent practice, have students complete page 113.

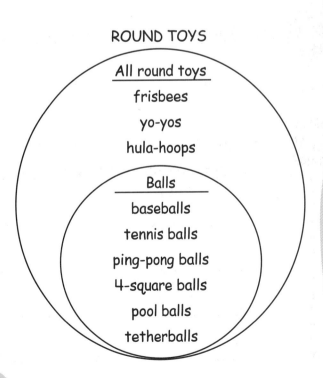

ROUND TOYS

All round toys
frisbees
yo-yos
hula-hoops

Balls
baseballs
tennis balls
ping-pong balls
4-square balls
pool balls
tetherballs

7

I am round. I am a toy.

You hold me in your hand. I have a long string. I go down and up.

What Am I?

Up and Down

1 Choose the word or words that <u>cannot</u> complete this sentence:

Yo-yos and basketballs _____.

are round	are toys	go up and down	bounce

2 How many other words can you write that rhyme with **toy**?

_____

_____

3 Which word is a synonym for **string**?

cord   ring   sting   wire

4 Circle the word that does <u>not</u> belong.

baseball   bat   hula-hoop   yo-yo

5 On the back of this page, draw a picture of your favorite toy. Write about why you like it.

_____

_____

_____

_____

113

Present the Riddle: Things

Remind children that the answer to this riddle is a thing, and that they should not give the solution to the riddle until you ask them to. Then follow these steps:

Use Picture Clues

- Ask a volunteer to name the living things shown in the picture. *(child, dog, frog, bird, tree)*

- Invite children to describe what is happening with the leaves and to speculate about what season this might be. *(Leaves are falling from the tree; fall or autumn)*

Use Text Clues

- Read the first sentence and encourage children to speculate about the sort of tool this might be.

- Read the other three sentences and ask volunteers to point out the text that gives them the strongest clues about what this tool is.

I am a kind of gardening tool with a long handle.

I have teeth, but I do not eat. You see me a lot in autumn. I help you put leaves into piles.

What Am I?

Answer the Riddle and Discuss Rakes

Invite volunteers to identify the tool *(a rake)*, and to share what they know about rakes.

Build Vocabulary and Concepts

- Lead children in brainstorming the physical characteristics of rakes, how they're used, and who uses them. Record their comments in a graphic organizer as shown below.

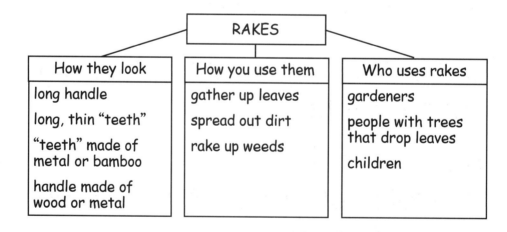

RAKES		
How they look	**How you use them**	**Who uses rakes**
long handle	gather up leaves	gardeners
long, thin "teeth"	spread out dirt	people with trees that drop leaves
"teeth" made of metal or bamboo	rake up weeds	children
handle made of wood or metal		

- For independent practice, have students complete page 116.

8

What Am I?
A Kite

Present the Riddle: Things
Remind children that the answer to this riddle is a thing, and that they should not give the solution to the riddle until you ask them to. Then follow these steps:

Use Picture Clues
- Invite a volunteer to describe what is happening in the picture. *(The wind is blowing.)*

- Ask children if the picture gives them enough information to guess what the answer to this riddle will be. *(probably not)* Record any hypotheses children have.

Use Text Clues
- Have a volunteer read the words spoken by the wind, then encourage children to revise their hypotheses.

- Read the first sentence; review and revise hypotheses again.

- Read the rest of the riddle and ask volunteers to point out the text that gives the best clue about what this object is.

Answer the Riddle and Discuss Kites
Invite volunteers to identify the mystery item *(a kite)*, and to share what they know about kites.

9

WHERE'S MY FRIEND WHO LIKES TO FLY?

I can be made of paper, cloth, or plastic.

I can be shaped like a diamond. I have a long tail. You run with me. I like to fly on windy days in March.

What Am I?

Build Vocabulary and Concepts
- Lead children in brainstorming the characteristics of kites. *(how they look, what they're made of, and what they can and cannot do)* Organize information on an attribute chart, noting features that kites do and do not have as shown.

- For independent practice, have students complete page 119.

Look like this	Don't look like this
diamond-, box-, or fish-shaped	round
made of paper, cloth, or plastic	made of metal
long tail	short string
long string	

KITES

Can do these things	Can't do these things
fly	roll
dip	be thrown
soar	bounce
crash	

9

I can be made of paper, cloth, or plastic.

I can be shaped like a diamond.
I have a long tail. You run with me.
I like to fly on windy days in March.

What Am I?

Go Fly a Kite

1 Choose the words that <u>cannot</u> complete this sentence:

It's fun to fly a kite_____.

| at the beach | in a forest | on a windy day | with a friend |

2 How many other words can you write that rhyme with **kite**?

_____

_____

3 Which word is a synonym for **windy**?

breezy   cool   sandy   still

4 Circle the word that does <u>not</u> belong.

cloth   paper   plastic   steel

5 On the back of this page, draw a picture of a kite you would like to have. Write about where you would go to fly your kite.

_____

_____

_____

_____

Present the Riddle: Things

Remind children that the answer to this riddle is a thing, and that they should not give the solution to the riddle until you ask them to. Then follow these steps:

Use Picture Clues

- Invite a volunteer to describe what the woman in the picture is doing. *(sewing)*

- Ask children if they think this picture shows modern times or olden times, and how they can tell. *(olden times; the people's clothing, using a candle for light)*

Use Text Clues

- Have a volunteer read the words spoken by the girl.

- Read the first two sentences and encourage children to speculate about what the mystery item might be.

- Read the last three sentences.

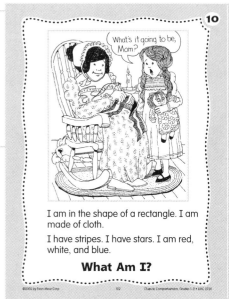

Answer the Riddle and Discuss Flags

Invite volunteers to identify the mystery item *(an American flag)*, and to share what they know about flags. You may want to tell students that the first American flag was sewn by Betsy Ross in 1776. Betsy Ross had her own business, upholstering furniture and sewing. She went to the same church as George Washington, and he was one of the men who asked her to make a flag for America. Betsy Ross was also the mother of seven daughters!

Build Vocabulary and Concepts

- Lead children in discussing the characteristics of flags, and of the American flag in particular. Sort their ideas according to characteristics that apply to all flags, and those that apply to the American flag specifically. Then record them in a graphic organizer as shown at right.

- For independent practice, have students complete page 122.

FLAGS

All flags

made of cloth or paper

use two or more colors

include pictures, designs, or patterns

The American flag

red, white, and blue

stripes

stars

10

What Am I?
A Football

Present the Riddle: Things

Remind children that the answer to this riddle is a thing, and that they should not give the solution to the riddle until you ask them to. Then follow these steps:

Use Picture Clues

- Invite a volunteer to identify the location shown in the picture and the details in the picture that helped to identify it. *(a stadium; scoreboard, team flags, fans in stadium risers)*

- Ask children if they think this picture gives them enough information to guess what the mystery item is *(probably not)*, and record any hypotheses children offer.

Use Text Clues

- Have a volunteer read the words on the scoreboard to confirm that this is a sporting event.

- Read the first sentence and encourage children to speculate about what the mystery item might be.

- Read the next two sentences and have children revise their hypotheses.

- Read the last two sentences and invite volunteers to point out the text that gives the strongest clue about the identity of the mystery item.

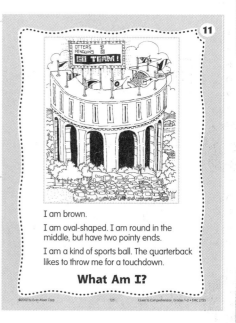

I am brown.

I am oval-shaped. I am round in the middle, but have two pointy ends.

I am a kind of sports ball. The quarterback likes to throw me for a touchdown.

What Am I?

Answer the Riddle and Discuss Footballs

Invite volunteers to identify the mystery item *(a football)*, and to share what they know about footballs.

Build Vocabulary and Concepts

- Guide children in comparing footballs and another kind of ball, such as a soccer ball. Record differences in their characteristics on a comparison chart as shown below.

	Shape	Color	How you use it	Where it's used
football	oval, round in the middle, pointy ends	brown	kick it, throw it, run with it	United States
soccer ball	round	black and white	kick it; hit it with your head or your body, but not your hands	all over the world

- For independent practice, have students complete page 125.

11

I am brown.

I am oval-shaped. I am round in the middle, but have two pointy ends.

I am a kind of sports ball. The quarterback likes to throw me for a touchdown.

What Am I?

Clues to Comprehension, Grades 1–2 • EMC 2720

Touchdown!

1 Choose the words that <u>cannot</u> complete this sentence:

When you play football, you can _____.

| bat the ball | kick the ball | run with the ball | score a touchdown |

2 How many other words can you write that rhyme with **ball**?

_____

_____

3 Which word is an antonym for **pointy**?

painted   flat   sharp   long

4 Circle the word that does <u>not</u> belong.

basketball   football   golf   wrestling

5 Would you rather watch football or play football? On the back of this page, draw a picture of yourself at a football game. Write about whether you are watching or playing, and why.

_____

_____

_____

Present the Riddle: Things

Remind children that the answer to this riddle is a thing, and that they should not give the solution to the riddle until you ask them to. Then follow these steps:

Use Picture Clues

- Ask a volunteer to describe what the bunny is doing, and what the expression on his face shows. *(checking the time; worry, concern, or surprise)*

- Ask children if they think this picture gives them enough information to guess what the mystery item is *(probably not)*, and record any hypotheses children offer.

Use Text Clues

- Read the first sentence and encourage children to speculate about what the mystery item might be.

- Read the second sentence and have children revise their hypotheses.

- Read the last three sentences and invite volunteers to point out the text that gives the strongest clue about the identity of the mystery item.

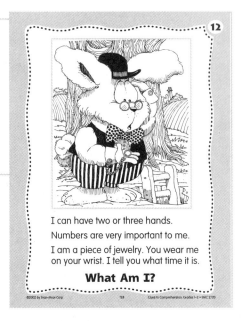

I can have two or three hands.
Numbers are very important to me.
I am a piece of jewelry. You wear me on your wrist. I tell you what time it is.

What Am I?

Answer the Riddle and Discuss Watches

Invite volunteers to identify the mystery item *(a watch)*, and to share what they know about watches. You may need to remind children that all watches have an hour hand and a minute hand, and some also have a second hand.

Build Vocabulary and Concepts

- Lead children in brainstorming different ways to tell time. Record their ideas in a graphic organizer as shown below.

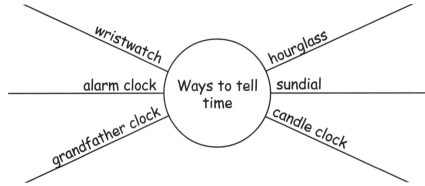

- For independent practice, have students complete page 128.

12

Present the Riddle: Things

Remind children that the answer to this riddle is a thing, and that they should not give the solution to the riddle until you ask them to. Then follow these steps:

Use Picture Clues

- Ask a volunteer to say what time of year this might be and what the weather is like *(winter, cold but sunny)*, and to explain what elements in the picture support these conclusions. *(bare trees, child dressed for cold weather, sunshine)*

- Point out the hat, carrot, and puddle, and encourage children to speculate about what they might be doing there.

Use Text Clues

- Read the first two sentences and encourage children to speculate about what the mystery item might be.

- Read the next two sentences and have children revise their hypotheses.

- Read the last sentence.

I am cold. You only see me during winter.
I am round. I am made out of snow.
Sometimes my nose is a carrot.

What Am I?

Answer the Riddle and Discuss Snowmen

Invite volunteers to identify the mystery item *(a snowman)*, and to share what they know about snowmen.

Build Vocabulary and Concepts

- Lead children in discussing what they know about snow. Record their ideas in a graphic organizer as shown.

- For independent practice, have students complete page 131.

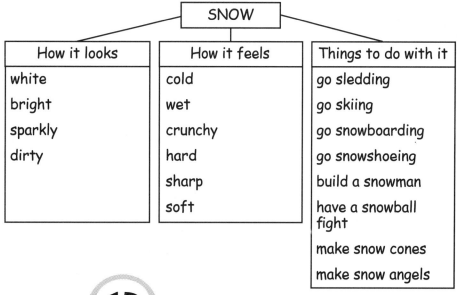

SNOW		
How it looks	**How it feels**	**Things to do with it**
white	cold	go sledding
bright	wet	go skiing
sparkly	crunchy	go snowboarding
dirty	hard	go snowshoeing
	sharp	build a snowman
	soft	have a snowball fight
		make snow cones
		make snow angels

13

I am cold. You only see me during winter.

I am round. I am made out of snow.

Sometimes my nose is a carrot.

What Am I?

ne:

Meltdown

1 Choose the word or words that <u>cannot</u> complete this sentence:

To make a snowman, you need _____.

| gloves or mittens on your hands   sand   snow   to be outside |

2 Circle the words that rhyme with **snow**.

know   no   now   show

3 Which word is an antonym for **cold**?

freezing   hot   old   wet

4 Circle the word that does <u>not</u> belong.

frost   ice   rain   snow

5 On the back of this page, draw a picture of a snowman you would like to make. Write about what you would use to make your snowman.

_____

_____

_____

_____

Topic & Details

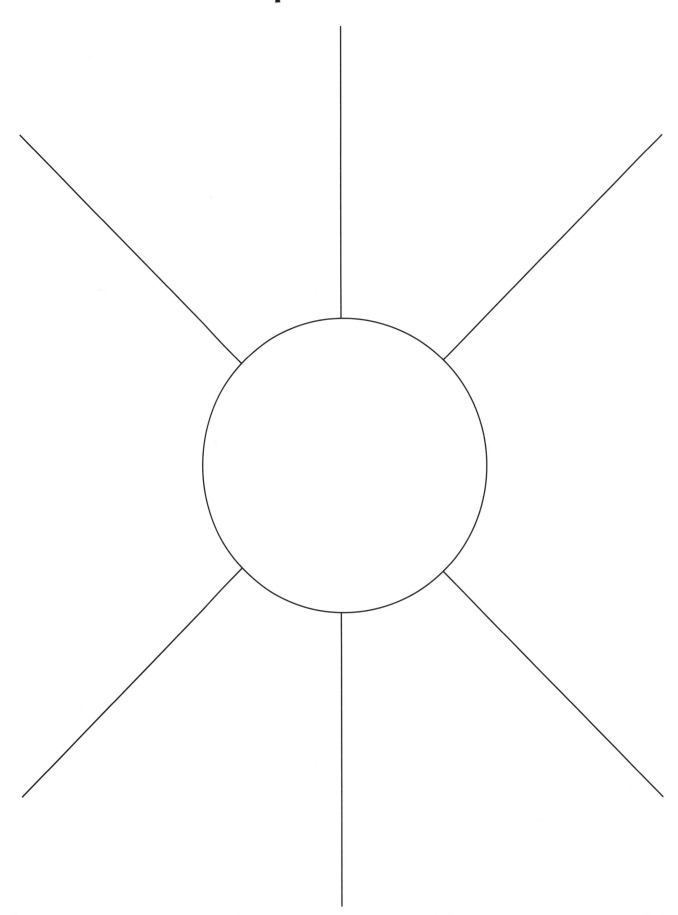

Topic, Subcategories, & Details

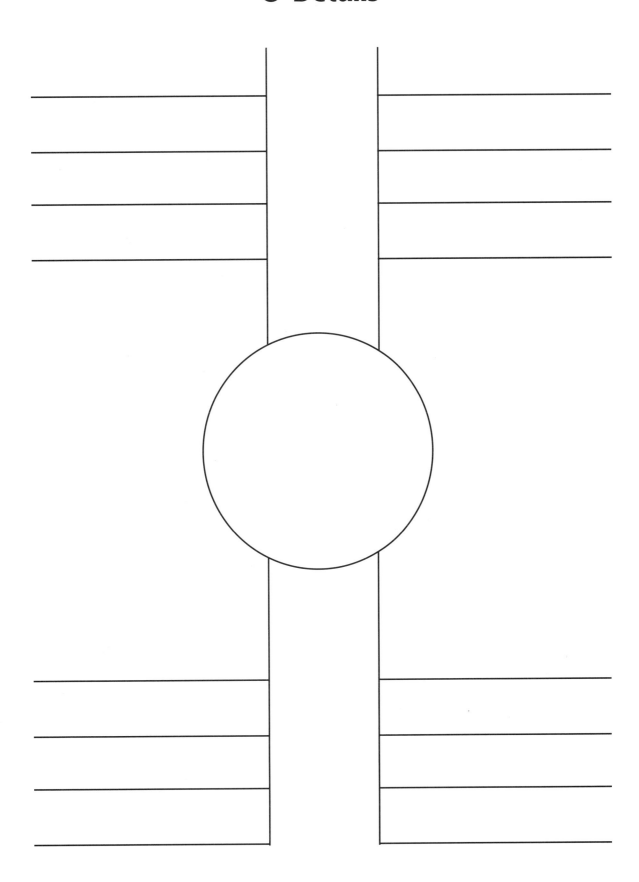

Topic, Subcategories, & Details

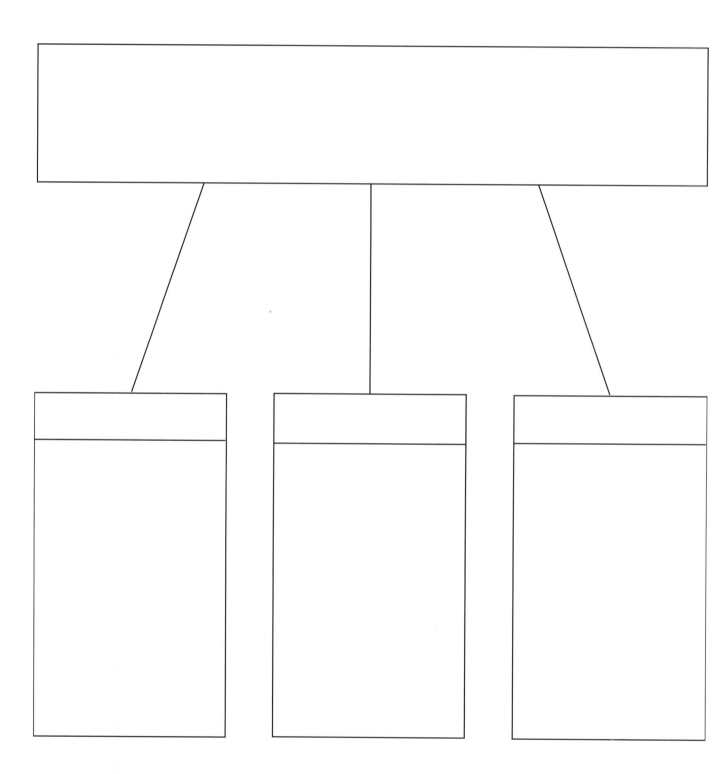

Synonym Chart

T-Chart

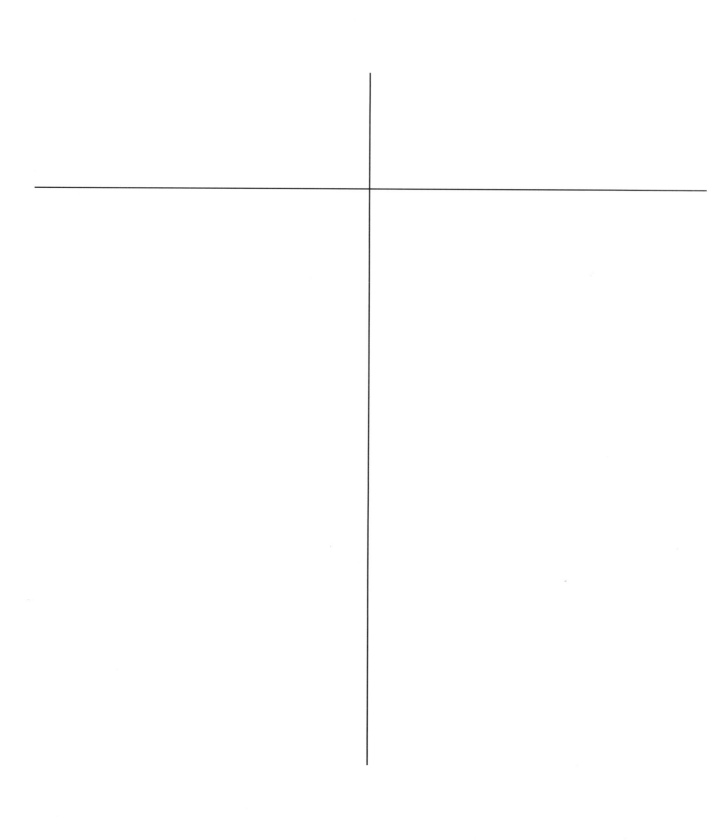

2-Part Venn Diagram

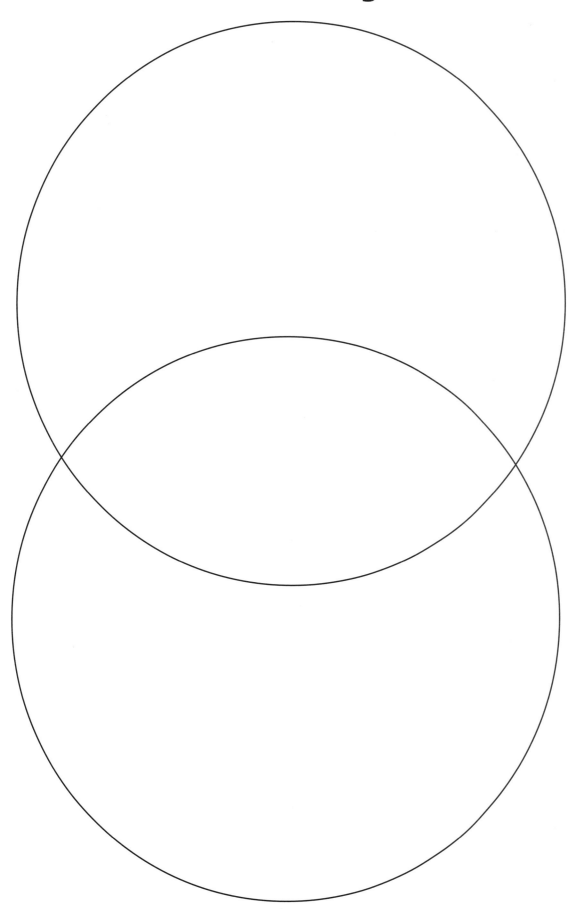

3-Part Venn Diagram

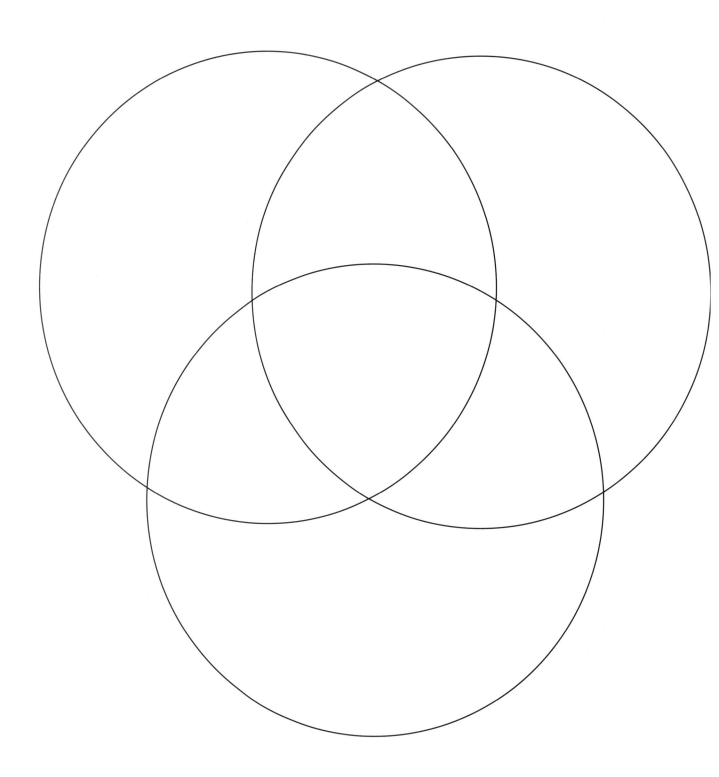

Comparison Chart

Set & Subset

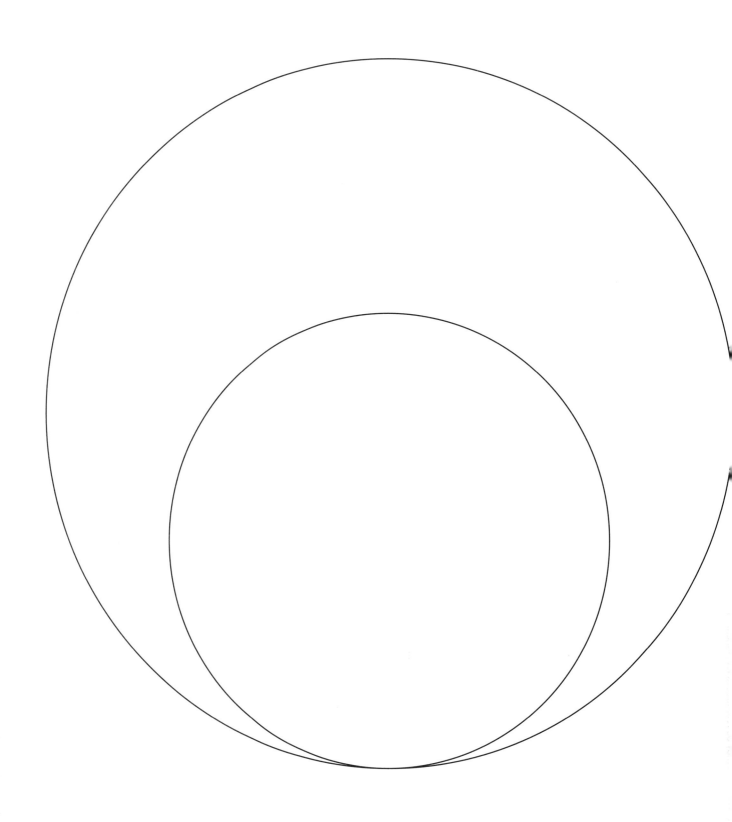

Attribute Chart

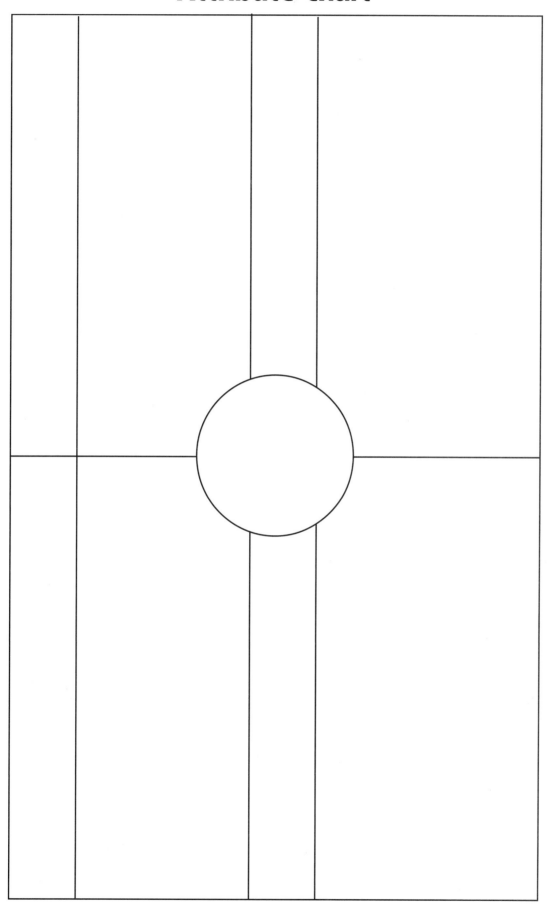

Answer Key

Page 12
1. sheep
2. Accept all appropriate responses, including beep, creep, deep, steep, etc.
3. bull
4. found
5. Answers will vary.

Page 15
1. a bed
2. Accept all appropriate responses, including ball, hall, stall, etc.; doll; bawl, crawl, etc.; haul, maul, etc.
3. barbecue
4. break
5. Answers will vary.

Page 18
1. well, fell
2. Accept all appropriate responses, including Bill, fill, grill, thrill, etc.
3. dish
4. hold
5. Answers will vary.

Page 21
1. inside the barn
2. Accept all appropriate responses, including bay, day, jay, etc.
3. zebra
4. trumpet
5. Answers will vary.

Page 24
1. "Not by the hair on my chinny chin chin!"
2. Accept all appropriate responses, including bin, fin, grin, thin, etc.
3. stone
4. woods
5. Answers will vary.

Page 27
1. Moon
2. Mom
3. a boy
4. near
5. Answers will vary.

Page 30
1. a tip
2. mood
3. cook food
4. diner
5. Answers will vary.

Page 33
1. a vet
2. booth
3. cast
4. pain
5. Answers will vary.

Page 36
1. sky
2. plain
3. sail
4. journey
5. Answers will vary.

Page 39
1. mail
2. male
3. truck
4. bring
5. Answers will vary.

Page 42
1. Firefighters do not work on holidays.
2. air
3. ladder
4. blaze
5. Answers will vary.

Page 45
1. clown
2. fun
3. engine
4. serious
5. Answers will vary.

Page 48
1. house, mouse
2. guide
3. seeds
4. present
5. Answers will vary.

Page 52
1. nature
2. Accept all appropriate responses, including dent, spent, etc.; meant
3. tent
4. indoors
5. Answers will vary.

Page 55
1. enjoying good entertainment
2. Accept all appropriate responses, including bark, Clark, shark, etc.
3. parade
4. concert
5. Answers will vary.

Page 58
1. energy
2. tickets
3. dirty
4. close
5. Answers will vary.

Page 61
1. train tracks
2. Accept all appropriate responses, including cane, Jane, lane, etc.; brain, grain, main, stain, etc.
3. calm
4. plain
5. Answers will vary.

Page 64
1. celebration
2. Accept all appropriate responses, including boat, coat, goat, etc.; vote, wrote, etc.
3. wand
4. Valentine's Day
5. Answers will vary.

Page 67
1. You can see dinosaurs at a zoo.
2. Accept all appropriate responses, including boo, coo, goo, etc.; cue, due, glue; view, etc.
3. tame
4. shark
5. Answers will vary.

Page 70
1. Students are paid to work at school.
2. Accept all appropriate responses, including cool, drool, spool, etc.; cruel, fuel, etc.; mule, jewel, ghoul, etc.
3. learn
4. vet
5. Answers will vary.

Page 73
1. a fancy restaurant
2. Accept all appropriate responses, including bay, day, stay, stray, etc.; hey, grey, oy vey, etc.
3. make trouble
4. jungle
5. Answers will vary.

Page 76
1. habitats
2. Accept all appropriate responses, including cot, dot, shot, trot, etc.; bought, caught, taught, etc.
3. cold
4. duck
5. Answers will vary.

Page 79
1. of vegetables
2. Accept all appropriate responses, including cake, fake, Jake, drake, shake, etc.
3. sour
4. steak
5. Answers will vary.

Page 82
1. wash clothing
2. Accept all appropriate responses, including hop, pop, drop, stop, flop, etc.
3. sell
4. jewelry
5. Answers will vary.

Page 85
2. Accept all appropriate responses, including bore, core, etc.; store, chore, etc.; floor, door, etc.; drawer, etc.
3. dry
4. freeway
5. Answers will vary.

Page 88
1. buy books
2. Accept all appropriate responses, including cook, hook, etc.; shook, crook, etc.
3. silent
4. postcard
5. Answers will vary.

Page 91
1. can look in the refrigerator for food
2. mood
3. chef
4. cake
5. Answers will vary.

Page 95
1. tame
2. Accept all appropriate responses, including bell, fell, etc.; shell, spell, etc.
3. friend
4. giraffe
5. Answers will vary.

Page 98
1. an insect
2. bait, gate, weight
3. trap
4. antennae
5. Answers will vary.

Page 101
1. help plant seeds
2. Accept all appropriate responses, including bop, mop, etc.; chop, stop, drop, etc.
3. tame
4. lemon
5. Answers will vary.

Page 104
1. eggs
2. bow, now, wow
3. ranch
4. beak
5. Answers will vary.

Pg 107
1. swim
2. heard, stirred, word
3. soar
4. snout
5. Answers will vary.

Page 110
1. in America
2. Accept all appropriate responses, including couch, ouch, grouch, slouch, etc.
3. leap
4. fins
5. Answers will vary.

Page 113
1. bounce
2. Accept all appropriate responses, including boy, joy, soy, Troy, ploy, etc.
3. cord
4. bat
5. Answers will vary.

Page 116
1. digging holes
2. Accept all appropriate responses, including: bake, cake, make, etc.; brake, drake, flake, etc.
3. short
4. water
5. Answers will vary.

Page 119
1. in a forest
2. Accept all appropriate responses, including bite, mite, spite, etc.; height, sight, fight, flight, fright, knight, etc.
3. breezy
4. steel
5. Answers will vary.

Page 122
1. in the rain
2. Accept all appropriate responses, including bag, gag, hag, brag, crag, drag, etc.
3. fabric
4. eagle
5. Answers will vary.

Page 125
1. bat the ball
2. Accept all appropriate responses, including call, hall, etc.; haul, Paul, etc.; bawl, brawl, shawl, crawl, etc.
3. flat
4. wrestling
5. Answers will vary.

Page 128
1. what time it is
2. Accept all appropriate responses, including dime, lime, etc.; crime, chime, etc.; rhyme, thyme, etc.
3. early
4. bracelet
5. Answers will vary.

Page 131
1. sand
2. know, no, show
3. hot
4. rain
5. Answers will vary.

Clues to Comprehension, Grades 1–2 • EMC 2720